HARTFORD

Photographic Moments of the People, Places and Lives in Our Region

HARTFORD

*Photographic Moments of the People,
Places and Lives in Our Region*

Gail Lebert, *publisher*

Keith Griffin, *editor*

Lynn Mika, *art director*

Moira Rosek, *project coordinator*

Cover photo by Leonard Hellerman: Statue of Mark Twain at the Hartford Public Library by sculptor James E. Brothers of Lawrence, Kansas. Statue was originally donated to the library by the Hollander family.
Back cover photo by David Newman: The Corning Fountain in the western half of Bushnell Park
Opening page photo by Steve Laschever
Previous spread photo by Riverfront Recapture
Left: The Genius of Connecticut originally sat on the dome of the State Capitol but is now inside.
Opposite: Tracks lead south from Hartford's Union Station which serves Amtrak, Peter Pan and Greyhound.

© Copyright 2011 New England Business Media, LLC

ISBN 978-0-9847039-0-6

Library of Congress Control Number: 2011941471

All rights reserved. No part of this work may be reproduced or copied in any form or by any means, except for brief excerpts in conjuction with book reviews, without prior written permission of the publisher.

Published by:
New England Business Media, LLC
Hartford Business Journal
15 Lewis St., Suite 200
Hartford, CT 06103

Publisher: Gail Lebert
Editor: Keith Griffin
Art Director: Lynn Mika
Author: Hartford Business Journal

Photography Consultant: Joseph Hilliman
Copy Editors: Susan Shalhoub, John Lahtinen
Advertising Director: Sharon Rozum
Special Projects: Donna Collins
Project Coordinator: Moira Rosek
Profiles in Excellence Writers: Jennifer Keck, Jane Weber Brubaker
Production Assistant: James Valentino

Distributed by Hartford Business Journal, www.HartfordBusiness.com

Printed in the U.S.A. by Taylor Specialty Books, Dallas, TX.
Jacket printed in the U.S.A. by Taylor Specialty Books, Dallas, TX.

The Profiles in Excellence were written and approved by the individual companies. The profiles may not reflect the opinions or editorial styles of the Hartford Business Journal or New England Business Media.

CONTENTS

Hartford: Photographic Moments
Greater Hartford's Story 8

Profiles in Excellence
Companies Founded 1635-1897 120

Profiles in Excellence
Companies Founded 1910-2006 166

Photographers 205

Company Index 207

Leonard Hellerman

Two of Hartford's iconic buildings, Travelers Tower and the Wadsworth Atheneum, framed by the lights of passing traffic in this long exposure photograph.

Hartford, Connecticut's capital city, and its surrounding suburbs, are an amalgamation of the best New England has to offer: culture, recreation, industry, history and a quality of life that is unparalleled. It offers four seasons of beautiful nature, outstanding academic opportunities from kindergarten through college — and a melting pot of people who make the region a celebration of the best in our world.

There's an obvious historical and literary quality to Greater Hartford when one thinks of the luminaries who were either born or lived here like Noah Webster, who penned our country's first dictionary; Katherine Hepburn, the actress; the Pulitzer Prize-winning poet Wallace Stevens; noted financier and banker J. Pierpoint Morgan, and, of course, the noted authors Harriett Beecher Stowe and Mark Twain. All have left an impression on the world that includes roots in Greater Hartford.

Yet, as the images for this book were being collected, something else became much more obvious. Greater Hartford is a place of vibrant natural beauty as subtly demonstrated in an image of a blue heron lifting off in flight from a pond at Goodwin Park in Hartford's South End.

Our region's beauty is also demonstrated by its parks and recreational areas. The symmetry of Hartford's history and beauty is, of course, best demonstrated by Bushnell Park that sits to the north and east of our stunning state capitol building in Hartford. The first municipal park in the nation to be conceived, built and paid for by citizens through a popular vote, Bushnell Park is a stunning example of our region's commitment to natural resources. As the

Hartford has a great love for its parades with their marching bands and celebrations of our heritage, service and successes.

PHOTOGRAPHIC MOMENTS 9

Fireworks illuminate the nighttime sky. Opposite: A coterie of cyclists are just a blur as they race along local roads.

Bushnell Park Foundation so aptly proclaims, "Bushnell Park today remains an oasis in the heart of the city where people from all walks of life come to renew their spirit and energy."

Another beautiful outdoor jewel is Elizabeth Park, on the border of Hartford and West Hartford. Its stunning rose gardens are a popular destination and must be among the most photographed places in Greater Hartford.

Outdoor recreational opportunities abound outside the city. The MDC West Hartford Reservoir and Reservoir 6 are outstanding venues for endeavors both sedentary and aggressive. Case Mountain in Manchester is considered among the best places in all of Connecticut (and probably Southern New England) for mountain biking.

Our most stunning natural resource continues to be the Connecticut River that forms the eastern border of our capital city. Thanks to the tireless efforts of Riverfront Recapture, this waterway that winds 407 miles from the Canadian border through Hartford down to Long Island Sound, has become a great source of recreation and entertainment. More importantly, Riverfront Recapture celebrates the diverse ethnicity of Greater Hartford and helps preserve and present cultural traditions through the programs it presents from spring to fall.

Even our tobacco fields, so artfully captured in these pages, have a certain beauty to them and are an important part of our agrarian history. The broad leaf tobacco grown here wraps some of the finest cigars in the world.

One element that has changed a great deal since last we published a photographic tribute to Greater Hartford in 2008 is how its people, places and things are captured for posterity and how those images are shared. No longer is it necessary to tramp down to the drugstore to process your film (which still exists somewhere we're sure). Now you simply pull your cell phone from your purse or pocket and point and shoot. Your image is instantly available for your world to see via Facebook, Twitter or other social networking sites. That sentence is one that would have been, at best,

Above and opposite: Hartford's annual Greater Hartford Festival of Jazz infuses Bushnell Park with a musical energy that lasts well beyond its four-day period.

just vaguely understandable three years ago but is now commonplace.

That's the reason this book includes a tribute to cell phone photography. It's an evolving art form that captures pets in quiet repose, the effects of Mother Nature (both good and bad) and gatherings of friends and family whether they are spread out on a picnic blanket listening to the excellent jazz emanating from the stage at Bushnell Park or celebrating one of life's milestones.

In addition to being an area of great natural beauty, Greater Hartford also showcases its beauty in its architecture both modern and historical. The Travelers Building is an icon of our skyline that continues to challenge and inspire photographers to capture from different perspectives. The Ancient Burial Ground, often overlooked by passersby, also has a reverence and elegance that call out to be captured for preservation.

The Wadsworth Atheneum, the country's oldest art museum, continues its relevance to art lovers as it undergoes a major renovation and expansion of its gallery space. It is but just one example of the many museums that dot Greater Hartford's landscape. Nook Farm hosts museums celebrating the Hartford lives of Mark Twain and Harriett Beecher Stowe. To the west is the Noah Webster House in West Hartford that weaves a historical tale of the man responsible for first chronicling the American language.

Slip even more to the west to Bristol where time is celebrated by the tick of a time piece and the sweep of a second hand at the American Watch & Clock Museum. Education subtly gets administered among children's sense of exploration also in Bristol at the delightful Imagine Nation that encourages the whimsical curiosity of children as does the whimsical Kids City in Middletown where children can explore and watch model trains in motion from a track side view among other special treats.

On the entertainment front, Greater Hartford is blessed with entertainment venues like The Bushnell, built in 1930

Greater Hartford as a community loves to honor those who have served and made the ultimate sacrifice through Memorial Day and Veterans' Day parades.

and later expanded to include the Belding Theater. Its main theatre features "Drama," the largest hand-painted ceiling mural of its type in the United States. Located just east of the State Capitol, the Bushnell continues to play host to major Broadway shows, symphony performances and operas. It has an annual roster of more than 350 events and an annual audience of more than 300,000.

The Hartford Stage, which celebrates its golden anniversary in 2013, continues to be one of the leading resident theatres in the United States. It is known internationally for its entertaining and inspiring presentation of a wide range of the best of world drama, from classics to provocative new plays and musicals and neglected works from the past.

The third piece of Hartford's vibrant professional theater community is TheaterWorks, an off-Broadway-style theater that produces unique repertory that addresses a broad variety of community issues. It is known for showcasing the talents of up-and-coming performers as well as established onstage and offstage Broadway veterans.

Finally no salute to Hartford is possible without the inclusion of its suburbs. The 35 towns that make up Greater Hartford are so much more than bedroom communities with their inviting retail experiences like Evergreen Walk in South Windsor and Blue Back Square in West Hartford. While Hartford is the epicenter of exotic cuisine, even our suburbs have embraced ethnic restaurants. The same can be said of the suburbs and their enthusiastic support of homegrown entertainment such as community theaters in New Britain and West Hartford, and even light opera in Simsbury.

So, if you haven't meditated on all that is right about Hartford, take a moment as you peruse this tome to remember all that makes this city and region the great place it is.

– *Keith Griffin*

Hartford loves celebrating the accomplishments of our beloved UConn Huskies who so often bring home national championships.

The hall of the state House of Representatives is both a popular spot on legislative tours of the State Capitol as well as the birthplace of landmark legislation that leads the nation.

Leonard Hellerman

Above: An interior staircase of the Wadsworth Atheneum's Austin House. Below: Hartford, by virtue of its long history, has government buildings that are not cookie cutter design, like the north portico of the State Capitol.

18 HARTFORD

Classic architecture reflected in a once revolutionary but now almost quaint glass skyscraper.

In the time of twilight and night, Hartford slips into an elegant repose that is both peaceful and beautiful. Above right: The clock tower in Constitution Plaza. Above left: The Phoenix building. Below: the federal courthouse.

Hartford, as viewed at sunset from the Northeast of town.

The sun set on The Hartford Times more than 35 years ago but its headquarters building continues to be a distinctive part of Prospect Street.

The "stilts building" on Church Street at night.

Leonard Hellerman

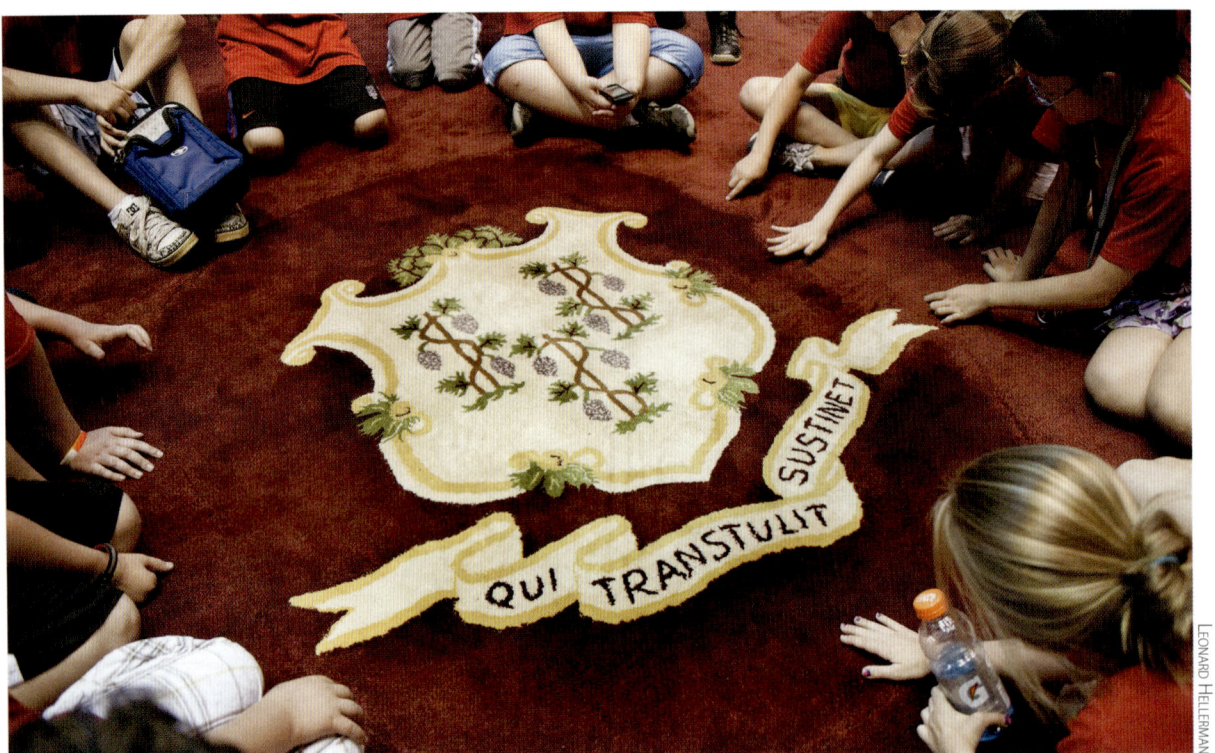

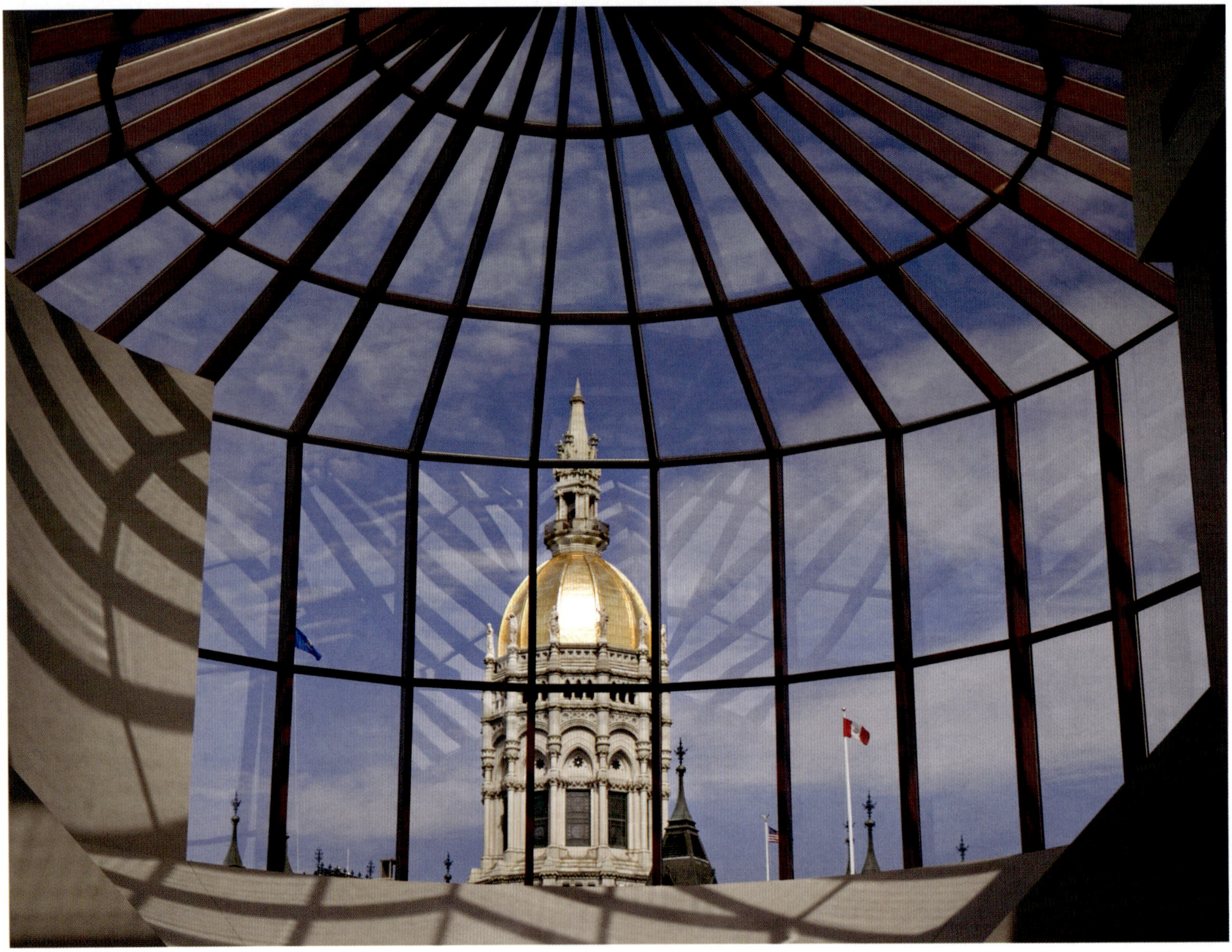

Leonard Hellerman

Various views both external and internal of the State Capitol, including the state seal, top, with the state motto that translates from Latin into "He who transplanted still sustains."

Looking up towards the dome of the State Capitol.

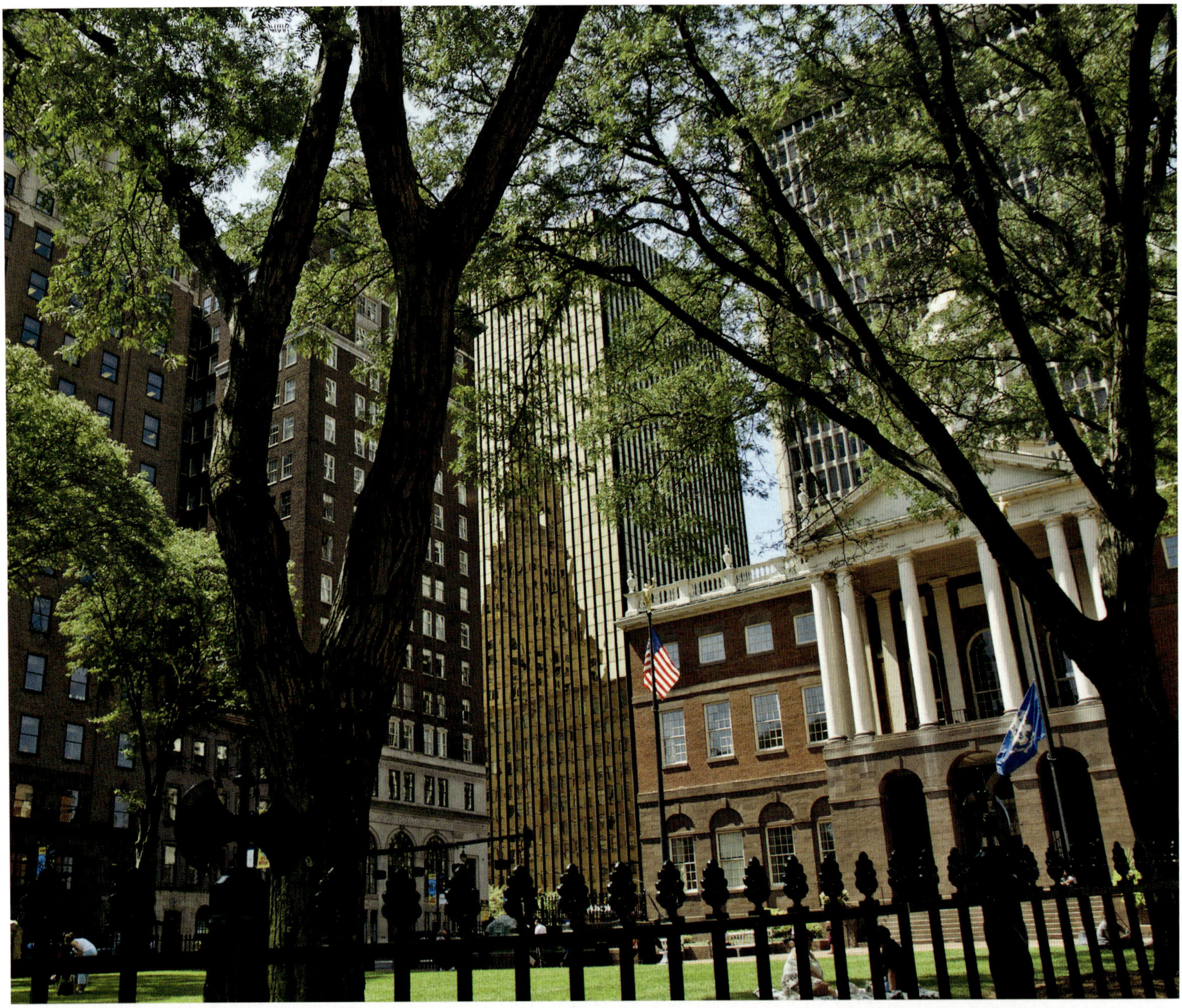

Leonard Hellerman

Leonard Hellerman

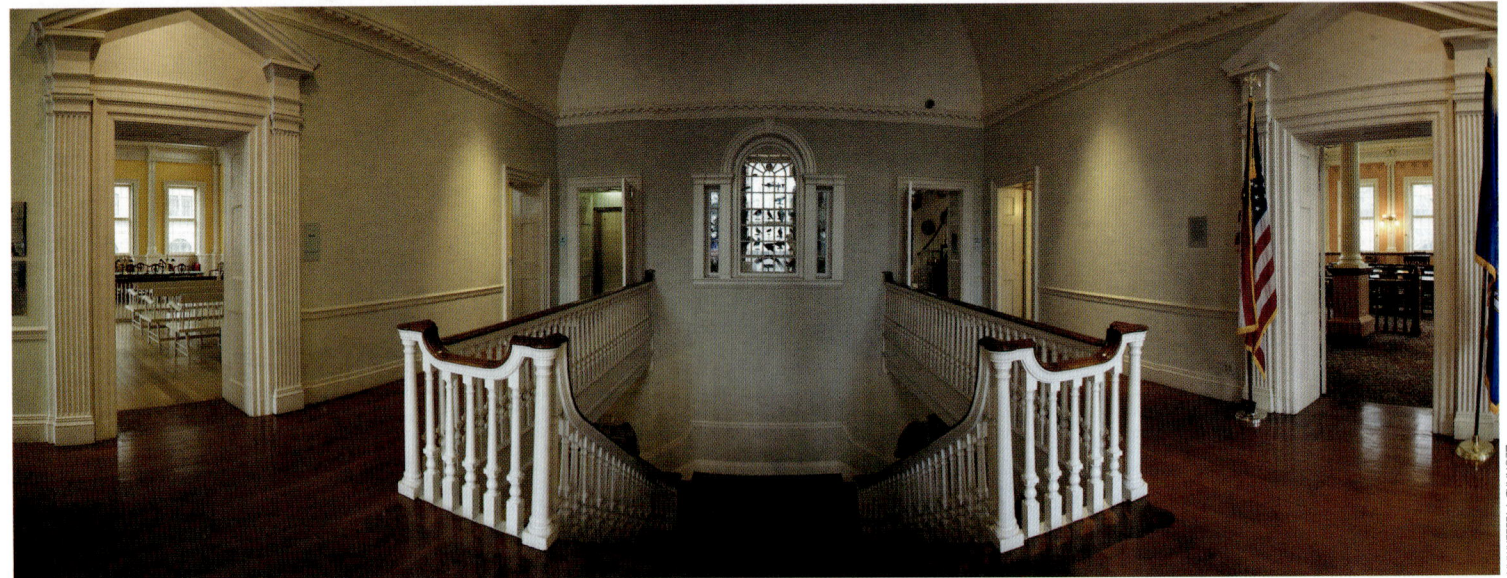

Above: As Connecticut's original state capitol from 1797 to 1873, the Old State House is regarded as one of the oldest remaining state houses in the nation. It is a popular gathering place as well as home to a historical museum and farmer's market. Below: The main staircase splits the entry into the judicial and senate chambers.

A statue atop a flagpole of PT Barnum, Connecticut native, circus entrepreneur and state legislator adorns part of the Old State House.

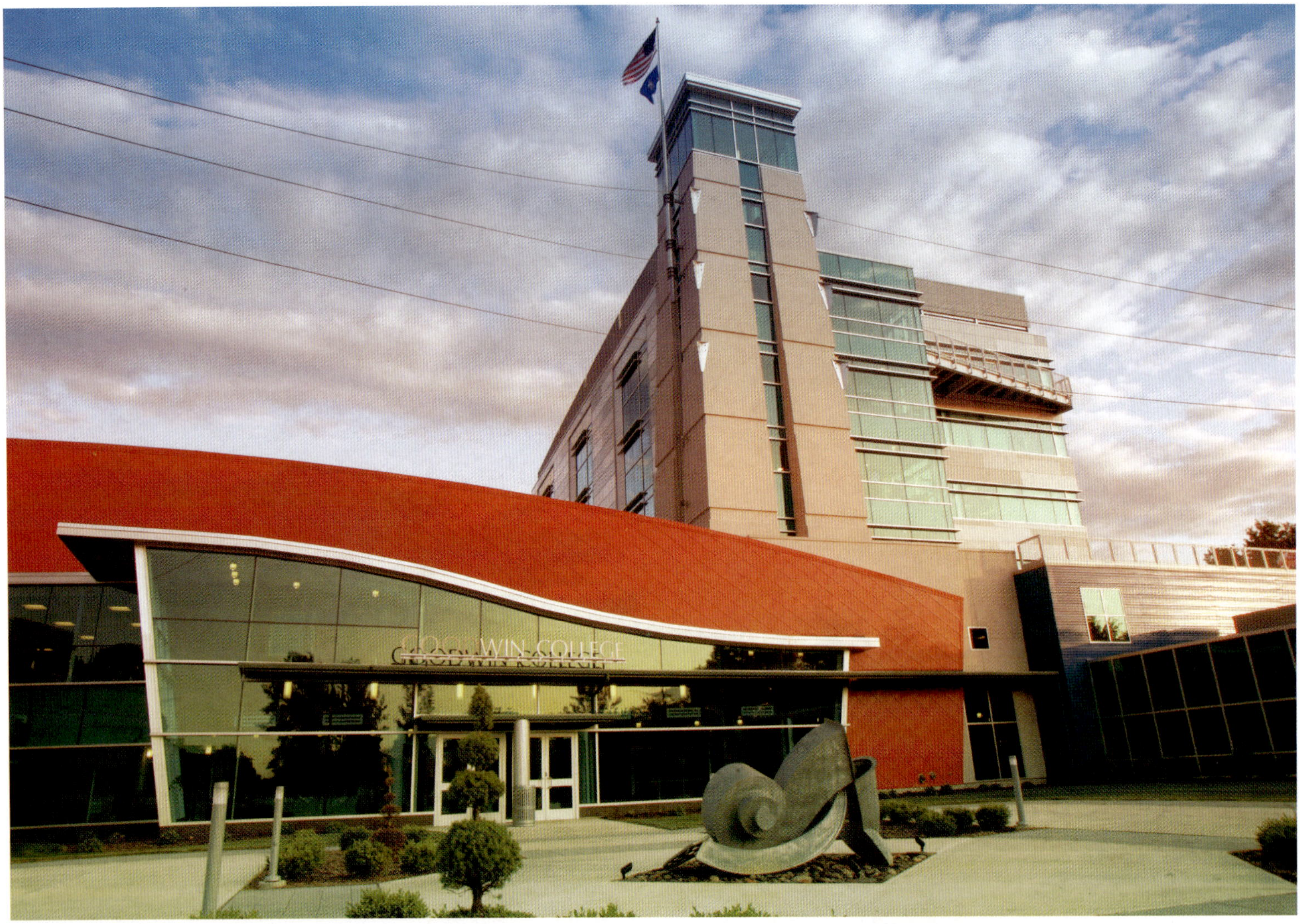

Goodwin College

Leonard Hellerman

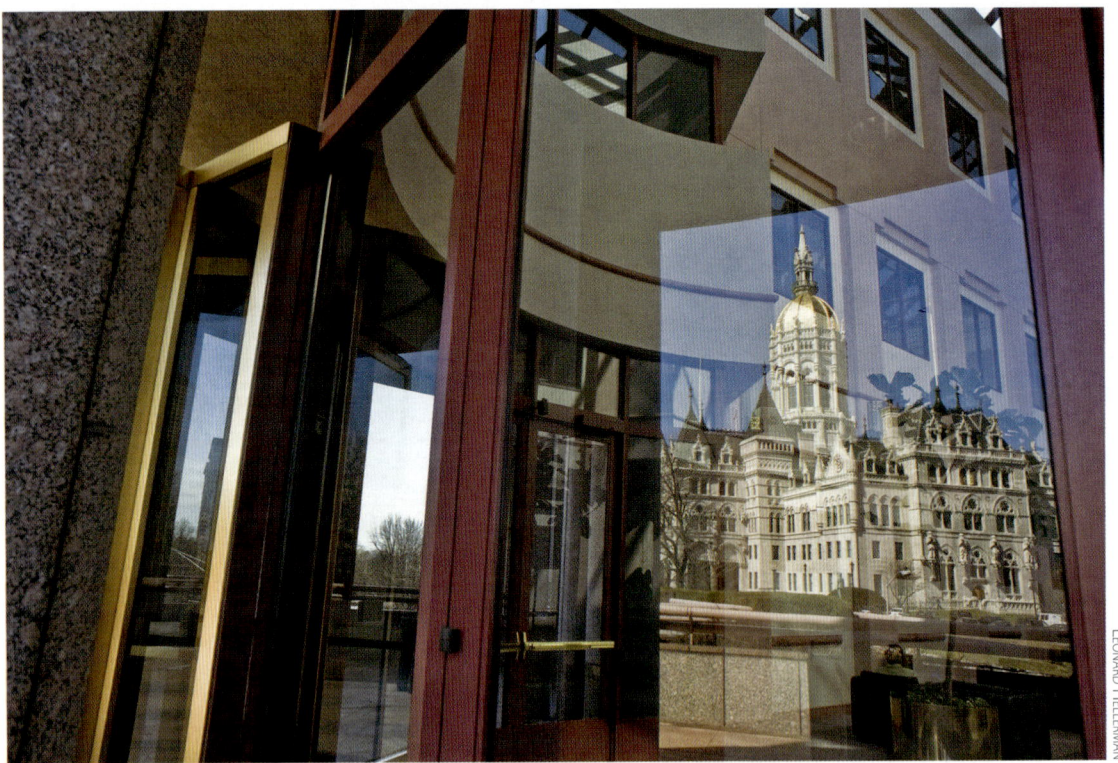

Top: East Hartford's Goodwin College. Bottom: the revolving doors of the Legislative Office Building reflect the State Capitol.

The restoration of a painting at the Wadsworth Atheneum.

This statue at Hartford's landmark Cedar Hill Cemetery portrays a woman in mourning, which was a frequent theme in Victorian mortuary art, according to the cemetery's website. The cemetery was designed by the same architect who created Hartford's Bushnell Park.

Trinity College in Hartford has beautiful exterior and interior artwork. Top: The cloister outside the Trinity College chapel is beautifully framed by a Magnolia tree shedding its colorful leaves in autumn. Almost all the doors that lead into the buildings on the Long Walk at Trinity have some carving or other as depicted here. Bottom center: A statue on the Solider & Sailors Memorial Arch that dissects Bushnell Park honors the 4,000 Hartford citizens who served in the Civil War, and the 400 who died for the Union. Bottom right: One of the many carvings from the pews inside the Trinity College chapel.

PHOTOGRAPHIC MOMENTS 31

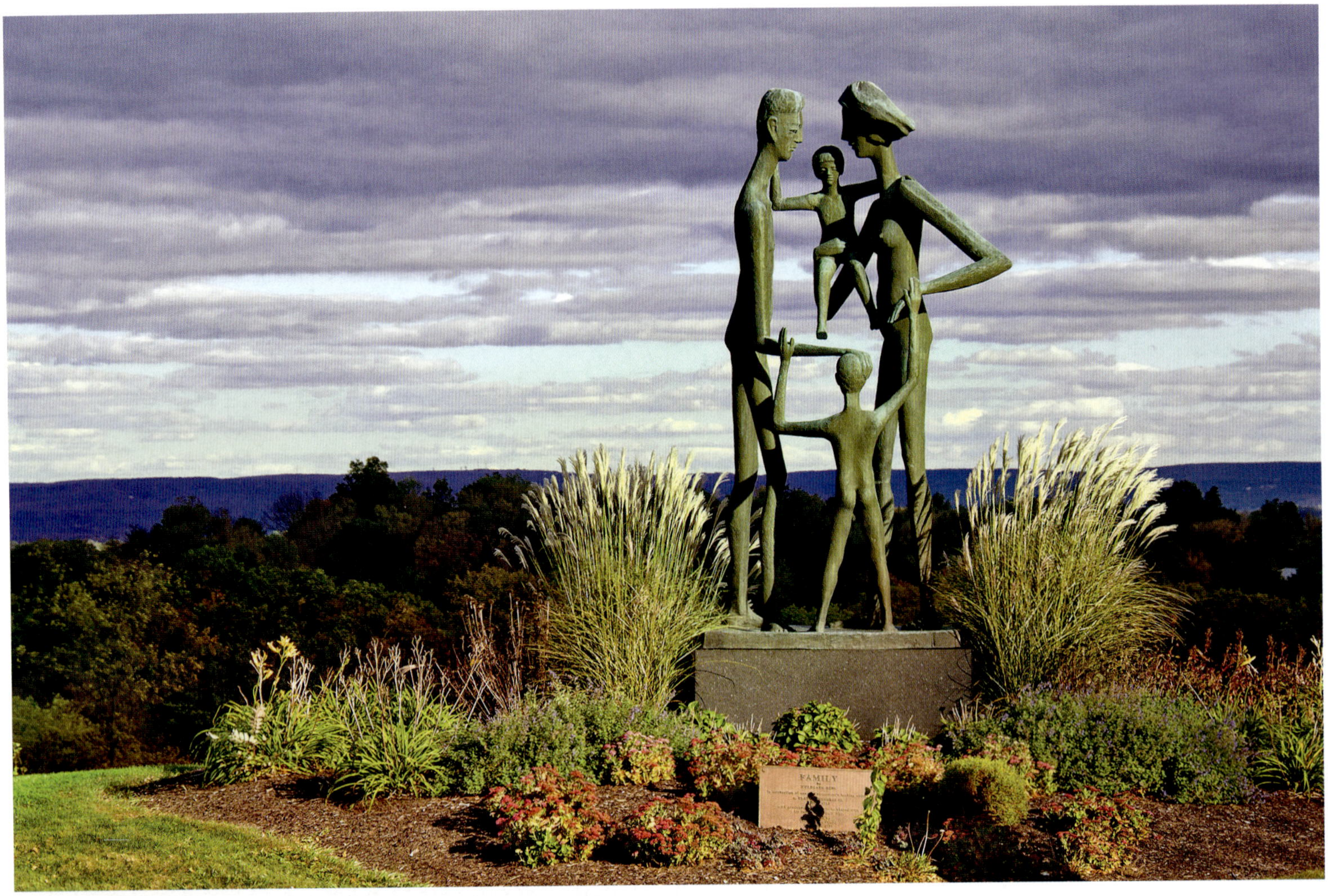

Leonard Hellerman

Kim Knox Beckius

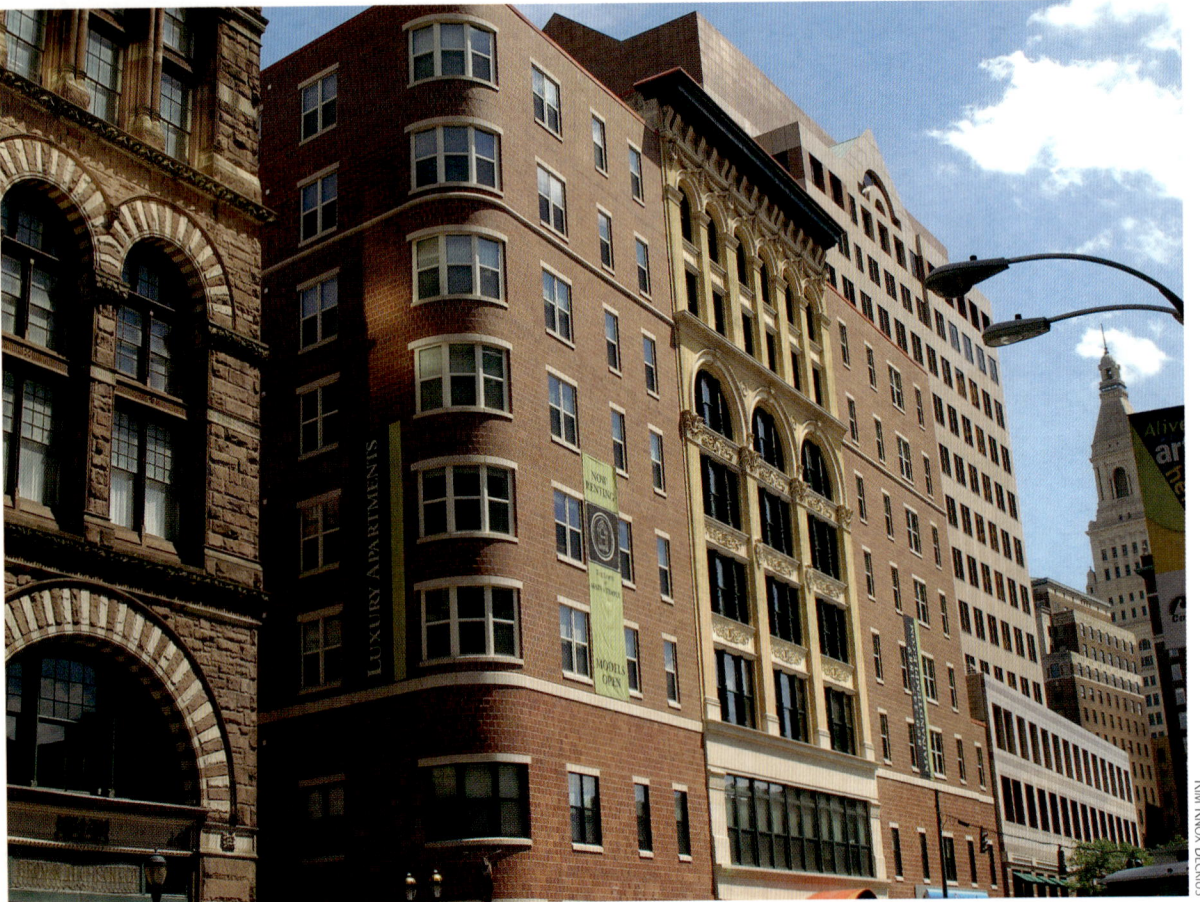

Above: This Wolfgang Behl statue called "The Family" was commissioned by the University of Connecticut Health Center in Farmington to create a work that signified the importance of its donors. The family in a circle represents the donors' support and caring for each other as well as the varied disciplines of the health center including healing and education. Below: Buildings along Hartford's Main street.

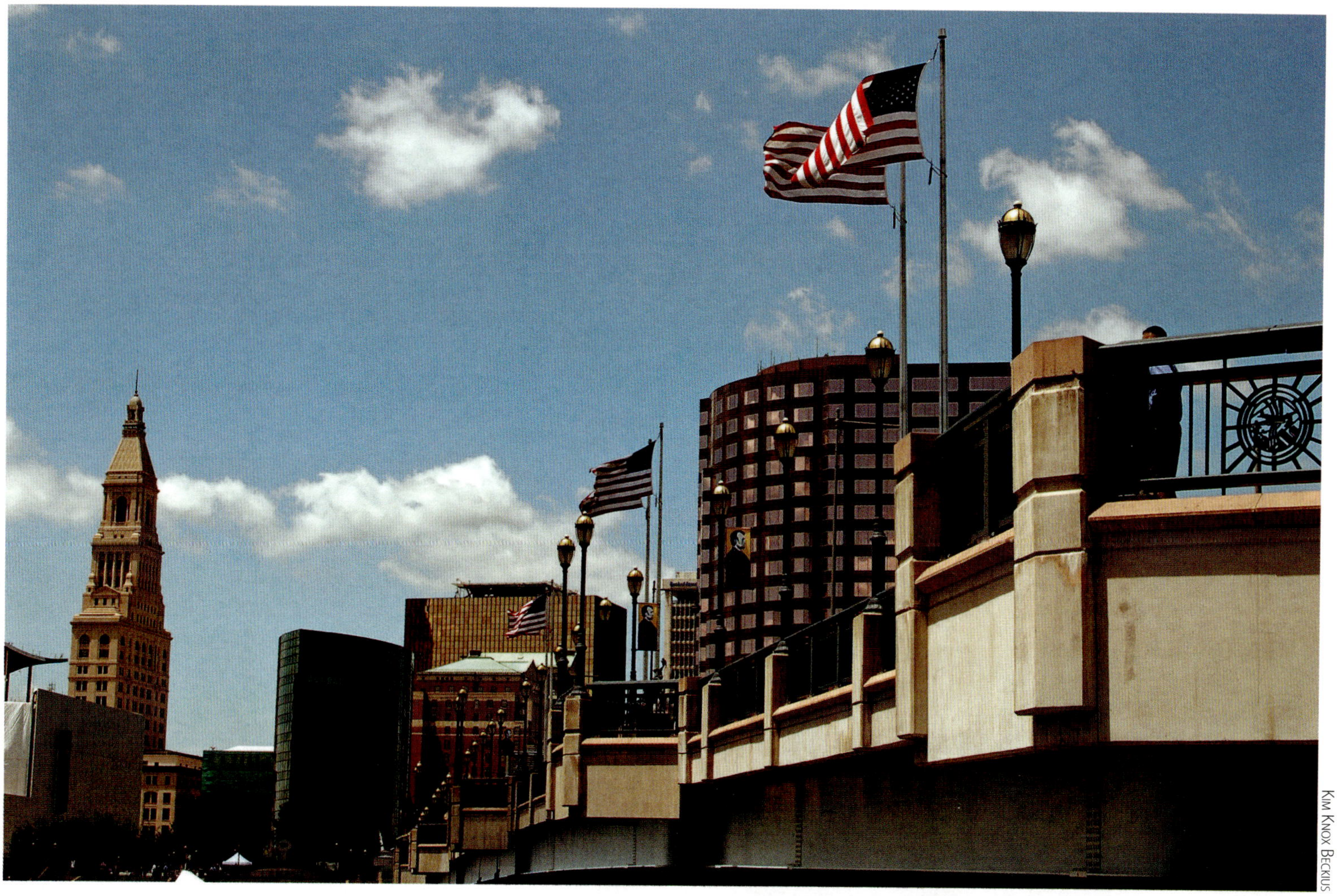

Kim Knox Beckius

Kim Knox Beckius

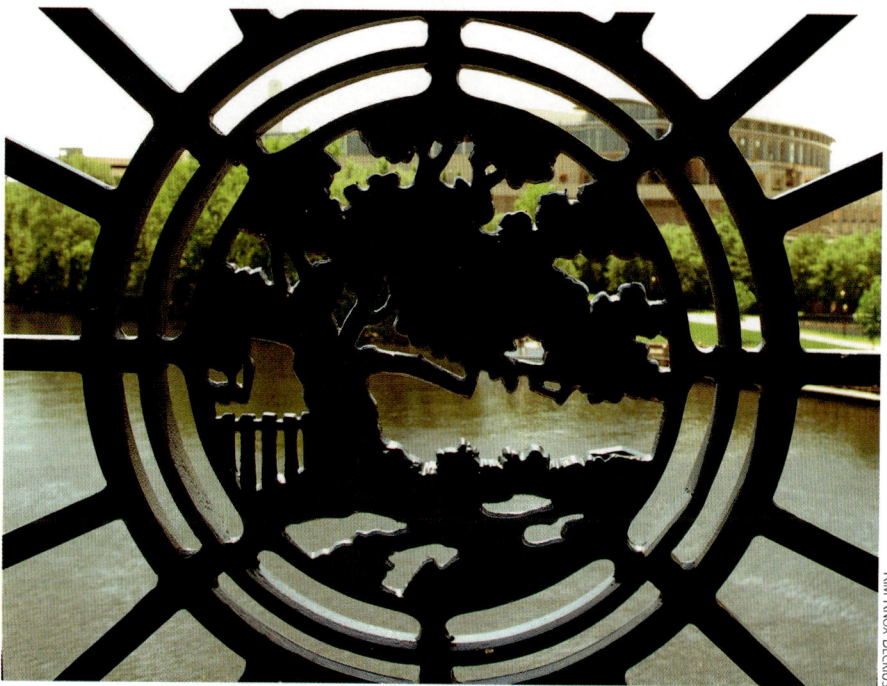

Flags flap in the breeze on the Charter Oak bridge which includes a close-up of the famous oak that once preserved our state's charter from seizure by the British government.

Perspectives of the Hartford skyline from the Connecticut River, the Colt Building and its watery reflection, and an ant's eye view north into Hartford from Sheldon Street.

Ongoing construction at the Wadsworth Atheneum.

Riverfront Recapture has done great work over the past 30 years creating what has rightly been called by visitors "an oasis in the heart of the city" that provides ethnic, athletic, family and musical events from spring well into fall. The organization has truly recaptured the Connecticut River for all to enjoy.

In 2007, Guakía, Inc. created The Ray González Latin Jazz and Salsa Festival, an annual event to honor the pioneering work of Ray González in Connecticut as a professional musician in Latin Jazz and Salsa and as an educator of the Latino youth. It is produced annually in conjunction with Riverfront Recapture and has featured some of the most talented international artists in Latin Jazz and Salsa.

On any given day in Hartford you can be regaled by jazz music in Bushnell Park, dance salsa along the riverfront, or enjoy a street fair.

Top: a performer at the Hartford Jazz Festival. Bottom left: Capturing a photographic memory. Bottom right: A stilt walker at a Caribbean festival.

PHOTOGRAPHIC MOMENTS **39**

Top left: The outdoor spaces in Greater Hartford provide fresh air that is enjoyed by the campers at Channel 3 Kids Camp. Top right and below: The parks also serve as host to both the dramatic wail of bagpipes and the appearance of an actor as Abe Lincoln putting forth his opinions on the United States during the Civil War to a rapt listener.

Equines, both natural and metallic, encourage a youthful curiosity and the ability to draw a crowd.

The "auld sod" descends upon Hartford annually in the guise of the St. Patrick's Day parade when the city is infused with green the Saturday before the March holiday.

42　HARTFORD

Above left: Who knew Mark Twain was a UConn fan? But it's possible because the University of Connecticut was founded in 1881 while Twain was living in Hartford. Above right: A young fan roots for the team. Below: The Husky mascot greets his adoring public during a parade celebrating the men's basketball team and its NCAA championship win in 2011.

PHOTOGRAPHIC MOMENTS   43

Flags serve both as patriotic reminders and heralds of our heritage.

Top: Flags are a poignant reminder of the ultimate sacrifice. Below left: Soldiers salute. Below right: A steel worker asks for silence as a steel beam from the World Trade Towers makes its way through Hartford.

PHOTOGRAPHIC MOMENTS 45

New Britain's Iwo Jima Memorial burns an eternal flame in memory of the hard-fought battle of World War II.

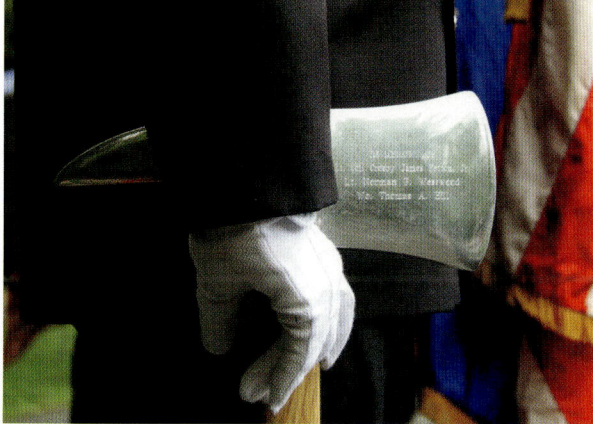

Firefighters and police officers gather in silent tribute to the members of their brave professions who no longer can answer the call to service.

Greater Hartford and aviation go hand-in-hand whether it's the jet engines made at Pratt & Whitney or the spacesuits made at Hamilton Sundstrand in Windsor Locks. Above: The New England Air Museum on parade. Below: One of the aircraft on display at the museum.

48 HARTFORD

Above: The New England Air Museum, located on the grounds of Bradley International Airport, the second largest airport in New England. Below: The LIFE STAR helicopter, a calming presence in our skies, serves a lifesaving function.

PHOTOGRAPHIC MOMENTS 49

Can you say Vrrrooommm? Motorcycles gather top and right at Motorcycle Mania in Middletown, which attracted 8,000 spectators amidst 4,000 motorcycles along Main Street. Bottom left: A classic automobile bears patriotic witness.

Top: Classic cars on display in New Britain. Below left: Antique cars parade through West Hartford Center. Below right: Street signs show all roads lead to Hartford (with the occasional detour).

PHOTOGRAPHIC MOMENTS **51**

Below left: Trolleys like those at the Connecticut Trolley Museum in East Windsor, above, continue to fascinate. Below right: Mighty locomotives that run along the western edge of Hartford from Union Station. Top: A child marvels at a model train set up at Kid City in Middletown.

52   HARTFORD

Hartford from north to south as viewed from a flight over the capital city.

People at work and play.

Top: The ING Greater Hartford Marathon is an Olympic qualifier. Below: Roller Derby demonstrates athleticism of a different nature.

Top: Baseball as modern youth call it or base ball as fans of the vintage version call it remains a popular staple in Greater Hartford. Below: When not rooting for the Yankees or Red Sox fans locally cheer our New Britain Rock Cats, the Eastern League affiliate of the Minnesota Twins.

Top: View of the 15th green at the Travelers Championship Greater Hartford's stop on the PGA tour since 1952. Bottom: The University of Hartford men's lacrosse team shows the winning style that resulted in its first-ever American East championship and a trip into NCAA tournament play.

PHOTOGRAPHIC MOMENTS **57**

Top: A dragon boat team prepares for competition on the Connecticut River. Bottom: The challenge of scaling a climbing wall is best accomplished one step at a time.

Thousands of fans turned out for the outdoor Whale Bowl at Rentschler Field that was highlighted by a game between AHL rivals Connecticut Whale vs. the Providence Bruins. Other highlights of that hockey fest were Army vs. American International College and top right a Whalers alumni vs. Bruins alumni game.

PHOTOGRAPHIC MOMENTS 59

There's a certain vibrancy to Hartford whether it's from murals, eclectic parties at Real Art Ways or a hip hop dance demonstration at the Mark Twain House.

60   HARTFORD

The Connecticut Business Expo is a premiere business education and networking event presented annually by the Hartford Business Journal at the Connecticut Convention Center.

Top: An Asian dance troupe at a South Elementary School in Windsor Locks. Below: A national touring production of "West Side Story" at The Bushnell.

Top: An off-Broadway dance number from "Shakespeare's "R&J" at TheatreWorks. Below: A local dance troupe in shimmering green outfits at Union Station in Hartford.

PHOTOGRAPHIC MOMENTS **63**

Youthful energy demonstrates itself in so many ways. Top: Field games at the Mark Twain House. Below: An art party complete with frames for self-portraits at Real Art Ways.

64 HARTFORD

Below: Kids have fun swimming at Channel 3 Kids Camp. Top and below right: The Connecticut Science Center, with its 150 hands-on exhibits, has been a strong draw to downtown Hartford for thousands of future scientists.

Top: The top of the Connecticut Science Center. Below: The view of the Connecticut River from the top floor of the Center.

Top: A sign at the Hartford Public Library demonstrates just how many different cultures call Greater Hartford home. Below: The interior of the Connecticut Science Center.

Vibrant colors pop at the New Britain Museum of American Art.

68 HARTFORD

Top: Alexander Caldwell's Stegosaurus glows orange outside of Hartford City Hall. Below: A kaleidoscope of colors cascade from the Hartford Public Library wall.

PHOTOGRAPHIC MOMENTS

Top: The Boys & Girls Club of Hartford could possibly be turning out future leaders. Bottom: Hartford Mayor Pedro Segarra.

Top: Gov. Dannel Malloy seen inspecting an historic American flag at the Old State House. Below: Girl Scouts diligently lower and fold the Stars and Stripes.

PHOTOGRAPHIC MOMENTS 71

Our history continuously comes back to life through fife and drum corps.

Top right: The Soldiers and Sailors Memorial Arch on Trinity Street in Hartford. Below: Civil War re-enactments and mock battles with cannon blasts.

PHOTOGRAPHIC MOMENTS 73

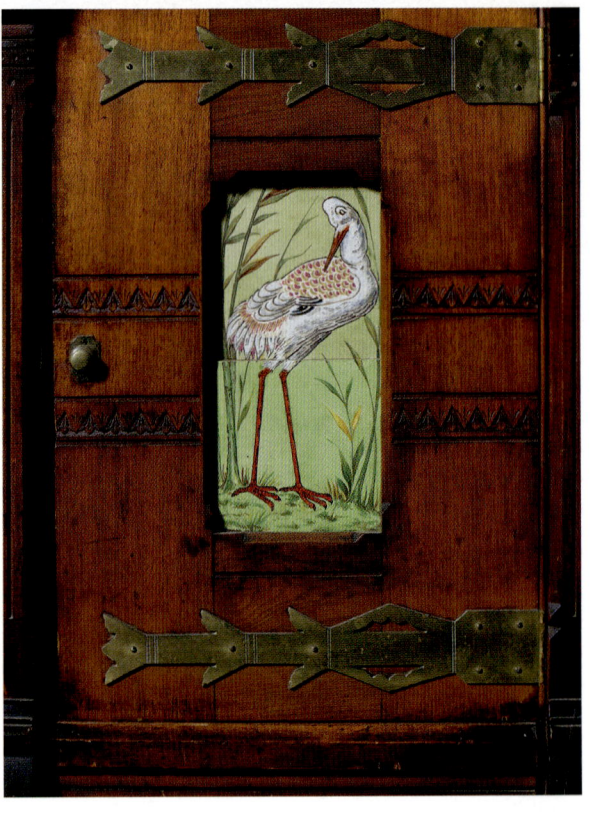

No book about Hartford could ever be complete without including its most-famous author Samuel L. Clemons who wrote under the pen name of Mark Twain. Top: His home on Farmington Avenue's Nook Farm continues to be a major tourist draw with regular celebrations that commemorate the life of Twain and his family. Below left: While obviously a writer of some talent, Twain's financial acumen was not as impressive; the Paige Compositor typesetting machine is what drove the family to the brink of bankruptcy, forcing them to leave their Hartford home. Below right: a door at the Museum.

74　HARTFORD

Scenes from celebrations and the interior of the Mark Twain House and Museum.

PHOTOGRAPHIC MOMENTS 75

The Wadsworth Atheneum was the first public art institution in the United States. It was also the first museum in America to begin collecting contemporary American art — resulting in a world-renowned Hudson River School collection. Also among its firsts was the first museum to stage a retrospective of Pablo Picasso in America and also the first museum to have its own theater, which is still actively used today. Top: Avery Court at the Wadsworth during the day is a quiet spot for artistic introspection but is a popular social setting in the evening for various charities and functions. Bottom: The Morgan Great Hall — previously home to the Wadsworth's collection of American history paintings displayed salon-style — has been reinstalled for the first time with large-scale works from the museum's Contemporary art collection.

Top: "Fishing Boats at Sea," by Claude Monet (1868), hangs in Hill-Stead's Morning Room. This is the earliest of Monet's paintings in Hill-Stead's collection, though it is the last Monet that Alfred A. Pope purchased. Below left: The Barnes Wing at The American Clock & Watch Museum in Bristol. It houses the museum's exhibit of tall case clocks that are often referred to by visitors as the "clock forest." Below right: "Grainstacks, White Frost Effect," by Claude Monet (1889), hangs in Hill-Stead's Drawing Room. On a facing wall, in the Ell Room, hangs the second of Monet's grainstack paintings in Hill-Stead's collection, "Grainstacks," in Bright Sunlight (1890). Alfred Pope, who met Monet, purchased the earlier work before Monet had painted the other.

Top: The oldest covered bridge in Connecticut is the West Cornwall Covered Bridge that has been in continuous use since 1864. Above left: A Suffield home built in 1805 by Thomas King. Bottom left: Memorial Hall in Windsor Locks. Bottom right: Heublein Tower atop Avon Mountain.

Top: Industrial remains. Below: A view towards Heublein Tower from Tower Ridge Country Club.

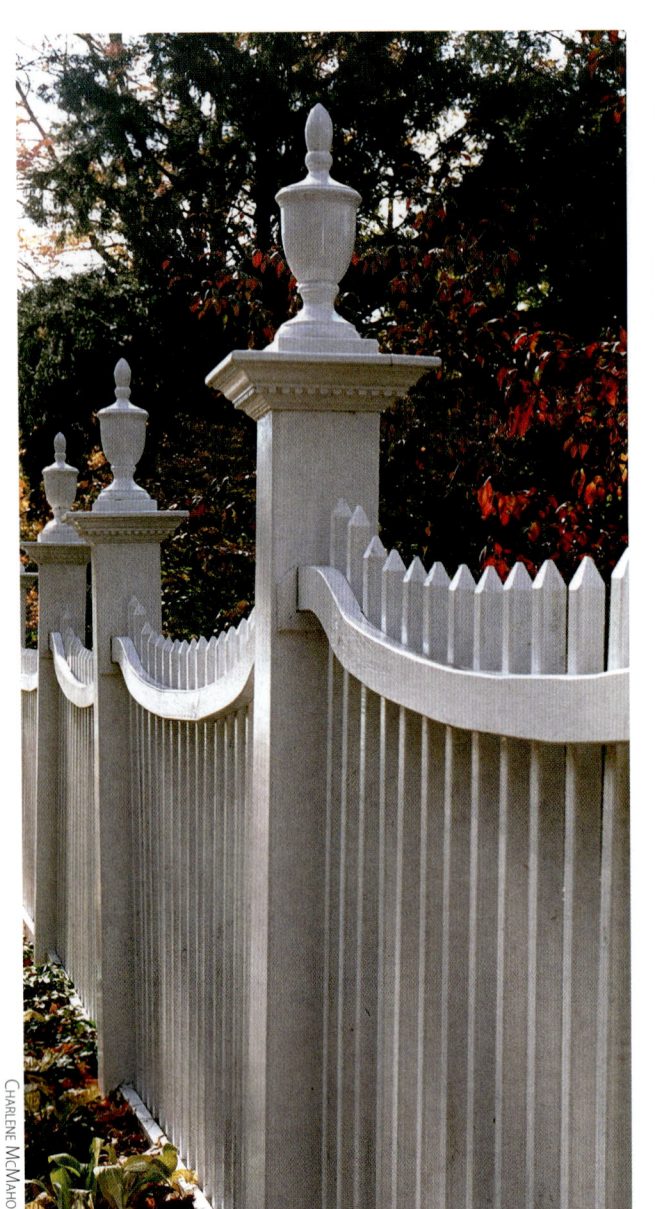

Idyllic nature scenes from around the region include a Blue Heron taking flight from inside Hartford's Goodwin Park.

PHOTOGRAPHIC MOMENTS **81**

Top: Glancing upon the brilliant colors of autumn in Ellington. Below: It becomes clear why Pulitzer Prize winning poet Wallace Stevens, who lived many years in Hartford, would compare the hues of fall to the Aurora Borealis in his poem, "The Auroras of Autumn" first published in 1948.

PHOTOGRAPHIC MOMENTS **83**

More of the brilliance of fall in Greater Hartford that is captured in a brisk autumn sunset that portends a beautiful tomorrow.

A tree, almost on fire with its intense colors, in the shade of a mountain. Below, one of Connecticut's many roadside stone walls watches a tiny sapling grow.

More photographic tributes to the autumnal hues from, dare it be said, a bird's eye view?

PHOTOGRAPHIC MOMENTS **87**

Is there any place more soothing to the psyche than the placid waters of a stream dotted with fallen leaves?

Top: The Pinchot Sycamore in Simsbury is considered the state's largest tree. Bottom right: Dipping a paddle creates ripples in the calmness that somehow help a kayaker achieve inner happiness along the banks of the Connecticut River.

PHOTOGRAPHIC MOMENTS **89**

Scenes from waterways like the Connecticut and Farmington rivers and their tributaries.

RIVERFRONT RECAPTURE

RIVERFRONT RECAPTURE

LEONARD HELLERMAN

PHOTOGRAPHIC MOMENTS 91

Nature provides inspiration in so many ways whether it's the painting of its beauty or the mingling of manmade objects with artificial props to make one stop in admiration of a creative eye.

A Farmington house decorated for spring.

Charlene McMahon

Andy Hart

Kim Knox Beckius

Visual textures take many forms: from a knitted sweater, to window condensation, to flowers and brick walls. The great English leader Winston Churchill sums up the feelings one gets when viewing these images: "I cannot pretend to be impartial about the colors. I rejoice with the brilliant ones, and am genuinely sorry for the poor browns." Fortunately no poor browns adorn these stunning photos.

LEONARD HELLERMAN

JOHN MURPHY

PHOTOGRAPHIC MOMENTS **95**

Agriculture is an important part of Greater Hartford, even with our designation as The Insurance Capital of the World not that long ago.

Kim Knox Beckius

Lisa Mikulski

Leonard Hellerman

More than 13 percent of Connecticut is devoted to farming with one fourth of the state's agricultural output coming from Hartford County alone.

PHOTOGRAPHIC MOMENTS 97

Wildlife both real and artistic makes us pause as we travel the back roads around Greater Hartford.

98 HARTFORD

Up close and personal with the buildings of a barn and the inhabitants of a poultry farm.

What better symbolizes the transition from autumn to winter than the abundance of pumpkins in a farmer's field just lying there waiting to be brought home for decoration.

Top: A pumpkin serves as a tasty treat for a squirrel.

Shade tobacco has been an important part of Connecticut's agricultural output for decades with the final product grown used as wrappers for some of the finest cigars in the world. Many farms survive in spite of many more being lost over the years to real estate development.

Far removed from traditional tobacco strongholds down South, one could wonder why Connecticut and more specifically northern Hartford County is so well known for its shade tobacco. It's for the same reason folks like living here: good soil, the right amount of rainfall, and lots of sunshine.

PHOTOGRAPHIC MOMENTS

Top: Girl Scouts thrill to gently pet a mighty steed. Below: a young 4-H member grabs some needed rest after tending to a prize sheep.

Top: Petting zoos are popular features of events like the annual Celebrate! West Hartford. Bottom: Animals of all shapes and sizes are typical at a Connecticut harvest fair.

Fairs in New England like the Hebron Fair pop up, blind us with brilliant colors, a cacophony of sounds, hunger-inducing aromas, skill contests and games of chance, and then just as quickly disappear not to return for another year.

Besides the rides, activities at the fair include eating funnel cakes and watching a demolition derby.

Mark Twain once said you could wait 15 minutes in New England and the weather would change if you didn't like it. Top: Sometimes, we can't wait for the rain to stop when it comes to an outdoor fair. Below: This sign along the river explains why Riverfront Recapture is so important to Greater Hartford.

108   HARTFORD

Quiet moments along the water's edge.

Since time immemorial, man has tried to conquer the water in many ways. That explains why we are drawn to events like a dragon boat race. Below left: A zip-line ride at Brownstone Exploration and Discovery Park in Portland. Below right: Racing a speed boat in competition on the Connecticut River.

110　HARTFORD

A quiet, reflective moment under a bridge while the world stretches out seemingly endlessly above.

PHOTOGRAPHIC MOMENTS 111

Nature rarely fails to make us stop and pause in her striking ability to create art out of just the right mixture of dramatic lighting and clouds.

Snowflakes, kaleidoscopes, slush covered cars and overweighted roofs. Yet, somehow, most of us still welcome winter when it first approaches in December. It's all part of the Greater Hartford experience.

PHOTOGRAPHIC MOMENTS 113

Top: A sudden ice storm or frost makes for a beautiful snapshot but it can have devastating effects on local crops. Below left: Cut-your-own Christmas trees are a huge part of the holiday tradition. Below right: Sledding on a saucer down a hill during school break in West Hartford.

Scenes of snow and ice from around Greater Hartford. Below left: The outdoor ice skating rink in Bushnell Park that was a strong draw in its inaugural season. Below right: A snowy vignette on Arch Street in New Britain looking toward South Church.

PHOTOGRAPHIC MOMENTS 115

Hartford Moments — As Captured By Cell Phone Cameras

The cell phone has become the go-to medium for capturing life's moments, which is why we publish select images of people, their pets, and favorite places from in and around Greater Hartford. No longer can most people say, "I wish I had my camera" because now it's as close as their phone. Memories live on thanks to modern technology.

PHOTOGRAPHIC MOMENTS 117

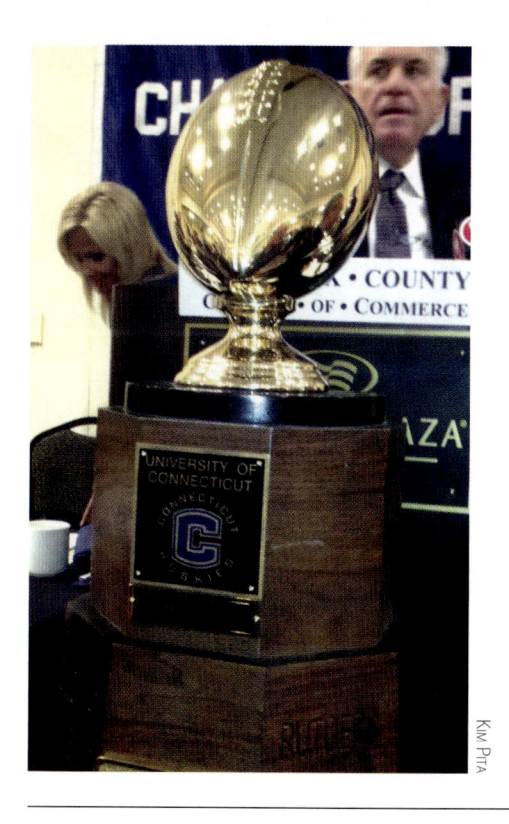

The atrium of the Legislative Office Building is a quiet and reflective place when captured in morning sunlight before the hustle and bustle of a day's activities commences.

Leonard Hellerman

Lynn Mika

Profiles In Excellence

The following profiles are a sampling of dynamic and vital business enterprises, professional service firms and institutions which bring prosperity as well as civic, social and human connections to our region.

Each organization has a story to tell, and it is here that they are told — in their own words. Arranged by their respective year of founding, these stories chronicle the strong commitment business and industry has exhibited — and continues to contribute — toward the well-being and quality of life in Greater Hartford.

1635-1897

Year Founded	Company Name	Page Number
1635	The City of Hartford	122
1764	Hartford Courant – CT1 Media	126
1767	Ahlstrom	130
1774	Hartford Public Library	132
1792	Cigna	134
1799	MetroHartford Alliance	136
1810	The Hartford	138
1843	Stanley Black & Decker	140
1844	McCarter & English, LLP	144
1850	PwC	145
1850	Aetna	146
1854	Hartford Hospital	150
1873	The Hartford Club	153
1875	Prudential Retirement	154
1877	University of Hartford	156
1881	Capewell Components Company LLC	157
1883	Northeast Utilities	158
1886	Charter Oak Insurance and Financial Services Company	160
1897	Saint Francis Hospital and Medical Center	162

THE CITY OF HARTFORD

The City of Hartford's story is a journey full of opportunities; a Who's Who and a timeline in history; and a remarkable feat of firsts.

Hartford's story is a journey full of opportunities; a Who's Who and a timeline in history; and a remarkable feat of firsts. First settled by the Dutch who set up a trading post and called it the House of Hope, it was later colonized in 1635 by the Reverend Thomas Hooker. Named after Hertford, England, Hartford, Connecticut is one of America's original cities. Thanks to courage, an audacity to be different and an adventurist spirit, Hooker and his followers made this city — and this country — great — because of the call for a free and open government.

"All power is to the people, and only the governed can govern themselves," he said. Today, Hooker's principles are reaffirmed. This is why Connecticut's Capital City stands strongly for civic responsibility, collaborative thinking, and not just positive, but groundbreaking and long-lasting results.

Hartford's legacy covers a national scope. Hooker's Fundamental Orders became the framework of the Connecticut Constitution — hence the name "The Constitution State;" Bushnell Park was designed by noted architect Frederick Law Olmsted and is the first public park in America; Hartford claims bragging rights to the first public art museum in the Wadsworth Atheneum; Hartford is the birthplace of Flag Day, which occurred two months after the start of the Civil War; and the Hartford Courant is the oldest, continuously published newspaper in the country and a living documentation of change in this city.

Evolving from an early agricultural economy, Hartford became an important trading center because of the mighty and majestic Connecticut River. Spices and coffee, among other products, were distributed from warehouses in the city's thriving merchant district. Ships set sail from Hartford to ports throughout the world. Hartford's insurance industry grew out of concerns about pirates and rough seas. Today Hartford is still known as the Insurance Capital of the World and The Hartford, Aetna and Travelers all call this "city of hope and opportunity" home.

Hartford has a history of being on the cutting edge of greatness thanks to inclusive partnerships. More than a century ago, the great collaborator Henry Ford came to Hartford to visit Colonel Albert Pope — the famed innovator and industrialist of Columbia Bike and Pope Park — to share some big ideas. Ford later said, "Coming together is a beginning. Keeping together is progress. Working together is success."

The spirit of the entrepreneur has also always been alive and well in Hartford. For instance, the "West Was Won" thanks to Samuel Colt and new techniques in manufacturing firearms. The Industrial Revolution brought prosperity to Hartford which meant jobs to a growing immigrant workforce. This ethnic and cultural diversity continues to be part of Hartford's DNA and is one of the city's greatest assets.

Three-hundred seventy-six years and 66 mayors later, Pedro E. Segarra leads a diverse city where 65 different languages are spoken as Hartford continues to be the Gateway to the New World, as it has been for generations of families. Touring Hartford is like taking a trip around the world. This diversity is celebrated and reflected through an ever-expanding showcase of restaurants, shops, arts and entertainment venues and architectural gems throughout the city's 17 distinct neighborhoods. Along Main Street is the oldest surviving building in the city — the Butler-McCook House

Above: The Colt dome during Hartford Riverfest ceremony.

Below: Historic drawing of the Hartford skyline as seen from the eastern bank of the Connecticut River, circa 1835.

—which traces Hartford's transformation from Colonial village to a center of commerce and government.

Hartford is also known as a literary capital. Great authors such as Mark Twain and Harriet Beecher Stowe were drawn to the area, called it home, and while residing here produced some of the greatest works that changed history. Twain once said of Hartford, "of all the beautiful towns it has been my fortune to see, this is the chief."

Today the authors' homes are two of the city's many museums and part of the historical architectural landscape. Other one-of-a-kind gems are the Soldiers and Sailors Memorial Arch, the Municipal Building — otherwise known as City Hall — and the "onion dome" atop the Colt Firearms building.

Architectural uniqueness is one claim to fame for the city. Another is that Hartford is an arts leader. The Hartford Stage, TheatreWorks, The Bushnell Memorial, and the Artists Collective are just a few of the long list of performing arts centers that produce and attract nationally-recognized and award-winning productions.

Hartford is now building upon its forte of taking the arts to the people. The *iQuilt* Partnership is working to connect or quilt together the city's cultural assets with its open spaces, especially the historic parks system. This effort builds upon investments to restore, beautify and replenish these treasures that have both regional and national significance. This system of parks is a blend of 19th- and 20th-century ideas, realities and inspirations that are being interwoven into 21st-century uses.

With the 21st century came economic challenges, but also an opportunity for Hartford to showcase innovative thinking that has always made the city great. Building upon strengths is a key to success. Thanks to the partnership with the Greater Hartford Arts Council, the Arts and Heritage Jobs Grant Program has invested millions of dollars into Hartford's Arts Mecca, a top-ten Arts Community in America. This means jobs. By retaining, expanding, and creating employment opportunities for Hartford residents — especially young people —the arts have proven to be more than good for the mind, body, and soul — they're

Above: View of the Hartford skyline today.

Left: Mayor Segarra with Archbishop Desmond Tutu.

Continued from previous page

THE CITY OF HARTFORD

good for the pocketbooks and cash registers as well.

Economic impact funding has meant millions of dollars in recent years to businesses, parking facilities, restaurants and the like. Hartford's 200-plus arts and heritage organizations are part of a center of commerce for a region of 1.2 million people, home to three Fortune 100 companies, and part of the job hub for the region and state. Hartford is home to more than 120,000 jobs.

Above: Mayor Pedro E. Segarra discusses Hartford's diversity during a special ceremony honoring the United Nations.

Below: Hartford student demonstrating excellence in science at the CT Science Center.

The job climate of Hartford's future will build upon the insurance and financial fields, medical research, and science as well as green and computer technology. At the core of this surge is education, where once again, the roots date back to the Reverend Thomas Hooker. Hartford Public High School, the nation's second-oldest secondary school, was established by Rev. Hooker in 1638. The building, now featuring four distinctive academies, is on Forest Street, in the former Nook Farm Literary Neighborhood of Twain and Beecher-Stowe. Hartford's commitment to reform and choice policies will continue. Consecutive years of improved test scores and five nationally-recognized schools will blaze the trail for even more progress. This again is the product of collaboration — parents, educators and businesses working together and investing in students.

Because urban areas like Hartford will provide 30 percent of the state's future workforce, it is essential that Hartford be a leader in higher education and be able to attract and develop dynamic, highly educated, and highly productive employees. As part of the Knowledge Corridor that runs from New Haven to Springfield, Hartford is home to Trinity College, the University of Hartford, the University of Connecticut's School of Business, the University of Connecticut's Law School, Rensselaer Polytechnic Institute's Hartford branch, Capital Community College and the Saint Joseph College School of Pharmacy. Rev. Hooker would be proud that the people of Hartford continue his pursuit of a better life through education and democracy.

That pursuit of happiness, by including the voices of the people, can also be seen today as Hartford marches forward with its *One City, One Plan* for conservation and development. This is an instrumental one-stop shopping plan of the city's vision for the next decade to be a global, green, and choice destination to live, work, play and raise a family. The goal is to create opportunities in a collaborative and inclusive manner in order to provide for a better tomorrow.

To continue to be an eyewitness to history, everyone is invited to embrace the city of Hartford via this book, technology and social media. Find out more about Hartford online at www.hartford.gov; follow on Twitter at HartfordMayor; and "like" the city of Hartford on Facebook.

Hartford is a city for the ages; a city of extraordinary history and progress; and Hartford is at the heart of New England.

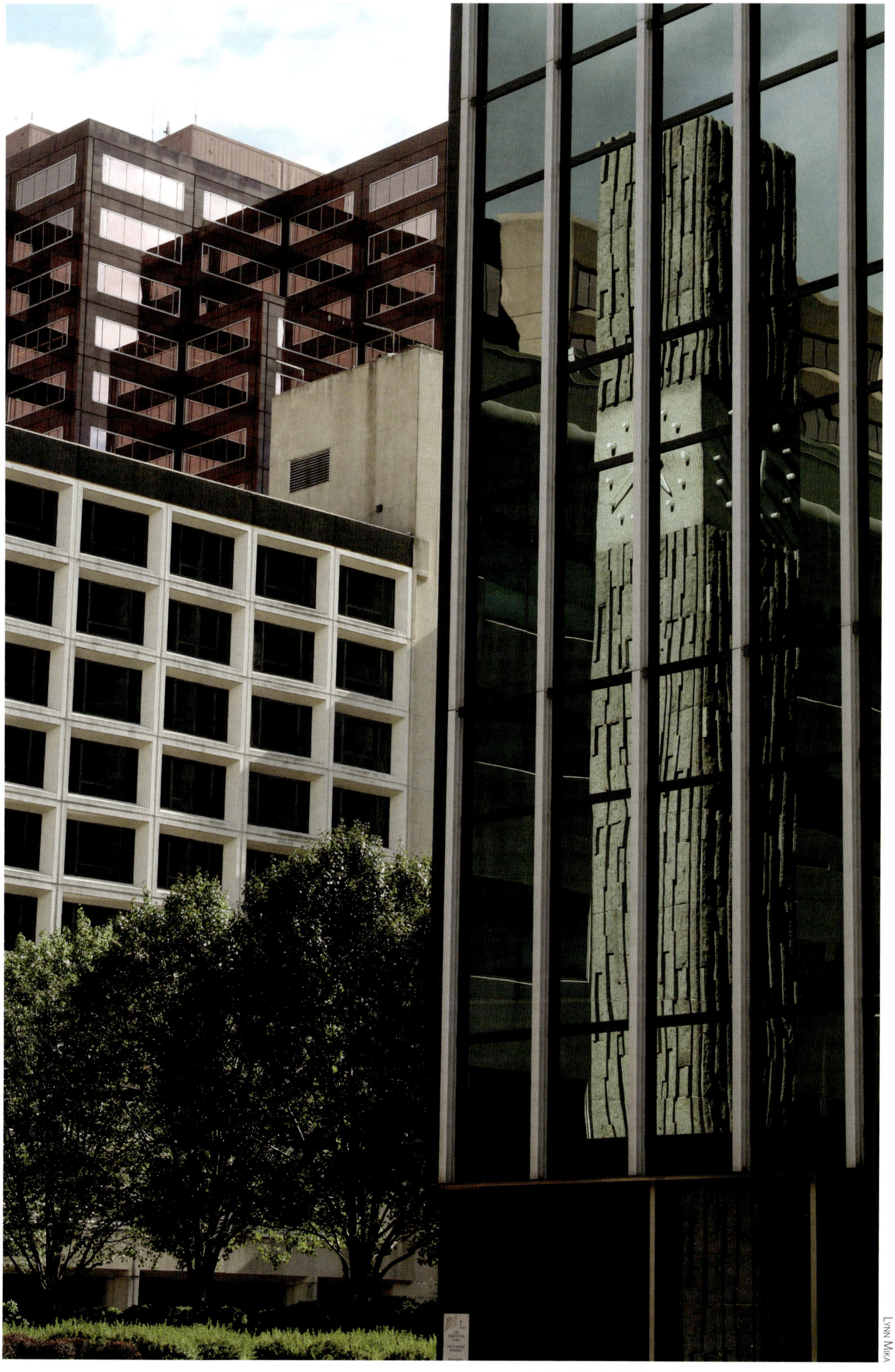

Lynn Mika

HARTFORD COURANT – CT1 MEDIA

CT1 Media's Hartford Courant/FOX CT newsroom is an always-on-deadline engine, keeping Connecticut residents up to the minute with the news and information they need to navigate their day.

The city of Hartford's founder, Thomas Hooker, was a fearless and charismatic preacher who, along with his followers, tromped through the wilderness from Massachusetts to Connecticut with high-minded purpose.

The Pulitzer Prize-winning Hartford Courant had Thomas Green, the resourceful son of a printer who — sensing opportunity — moved from New Haven and began publishing a weekly paper, The Connecticut Courant, in Hartford.

The Connecticut Courant became the Daily Courant in 1837 and was renamed the Hartford Courant in 1887. The Courant has never missed an issue since it was founded on October 29, 1764.

"America's Oldest Continuously Published Newspaper" is still based in Hartford, where you will also find the nation's oldest public art museum, the Wadsworth Atheneum, the oldest municipal park, Bushnell Park, and the second-oldest secondary school, Hartford Public.

In 1894, the Courant reached even deeper into the community when it opened a summer camp for children. Hartford's Camp Courant became the nation's largest free day camp, a title it holds to this day.

"We're proud to be in Hartford, a city as rich in tradition as the Courant," says Richard Graziano, the Courant's forward-looking publisher, president and CEO. Graziano is also the vice president and general manager of FOX CT/WCCT-TV.

"We are Hartford's own," Graziano says from his fourth-floor office on Broad Street, with the modern studio of Connecticut's newsroom one floor below.

Best of both worlds

When the FOX Connecticut television station moved into Broad Street alongside the Courant in 2009 under Graziano's stewardship, one of the most dynamic and diversified local media companies in the country — CT1 Media — was born.

CT1 Media combines the trusted, long-standing heritage of the Courant and the most technologically advanced TV news production facilities in the industry. Integration is at the core of CT1 Media's operations and content gathering, while its brands and news products exist independently to serve their respective audiences.

"CT1 Media is Hartford's media company," Graziano says. "It combines tradition and trust while delivering the most local news in the state from one of the most modern newsrooms in the country."

Fixed in history and the future

The Courant is the newspaper in which George Washington placed an ad to lease part of his Mount Vernon land.

Thomas Jefferson sued the newspaper for libel —

The Connecticut Courant The Courant has not missed an issue since this front page was printed in 1764.

and lost. Jefferson led the Republican party. Connecticut, a Federalist state, was one of only two states Jefferson did not carry in 1804.

"Jefferson would ultimately claim the libel cases were filed without his knowledge, but there is no doubt that, by 1806, he was sick of Connecticut and sick of newspapers like The Courant," the Courant reported in 1998. The libel charges were dropped in 1809.

Mark Twain, who was one of Hartford's "literate gentlemen" along with Courant Publisher Charles Dudley Warner, tried to buy stock in the paper but his offer was rejected.

"Twain had tried to buy into The Courant in 1869, before coming to Hartford," John Bard McNulty wrote in his book, "Older Than the Nation: The Story of The Hartford Courant." The Courant's owner at the time, Joseph Roswell Hawley, and Warner gave the proposal careful consideration but for some unknown reason turned it down. "Twain evidently regarded the refusal to sell a share of the newspaper as a personal rebuff, and for a while after coming to Hartford he treated Warner rather cooly. But it was hard to know Warner and not to like him. The two were soon collaborating on their novel, ["The Gilded Age"], and before long Warner was Cousin Charley to Twain's children," McNulty wrote.

Today the Courant is known for its exclusive investigative reporting on politics and government accountability as well as its sports coverage. The Courant is the go-to source for the latest on UConn and high school athletic scores, schedules and news. Although they are independent news operations, the Courant and FOX CT have access to combined resources — resulting in the ability to provide greater coverage of the local community and celebration of its diversity for readers and viewers alike.

The newspaper was honored with its first Pulitzer Prize in 1992 for its investigative reporting into the problems with the Hubble Space Telescope. In 1999 the paper won another Pulitzer in the Breaking News category for coverage of a multiple murder-suicide at Connecticut Lottery headquarters.

FOX CT is the leading local news gathering operation in the state, providing 46.5 hours of local news each week to viewers in the Hartford/New Haven market, more than any other station in the state. The station is known for its local news and event coverage, from New Haven's St. Patrick's Day Parade to the Hartford Marathon and the annual Thanksgiving Day Manchester Road Race.

CT1 Media also consists of New Mass. Media, the publisher of the

Above: The Hartford Courant iPad app puts the news at your fingertips.

Below: Richard Graziano, the Courant's publisher, president and CEO and the vice president and general manager of FOX CT/WCCT-TV, poses in front of a mural inside the CT1 Media building on Broad Street in Hartford.

Continued on next page

Continued from previous page

HARTFORD COURANT – CT1 MEDIA

Hartford Advocate, the New Haven Advocate and the Fairfield County Weekly.

In addition to its print products, CT1 Media publishes digitally on courant.com, ctnow.com and ct.com. CT1 Media also offers news and information through its mobile apps, including those for UConn Husky athletics, politics, dining and deals.

You'll also find CT1 Media on social media sites with daily money-saving deals, news feeds on Facebook and TV and print reporters posting news as it happens on Twitter. Print stories are published online immediately, often with accompanying video for richer, more saturated storytelling.

While television and print enjoy editorial independence, the combination of newspaper, television and digital reporting means more information about important news stories is available to readers and viewers. Together, these mediums form an incredible statewide news service. "CT1 Media is the only fully integrated newsroom, resulting in news gathering that is more robust, rich and detailed," Graziano says.

The combined Courant/FOX CT newsroom is an always-on-deadline engine, keeping Connecticut residents up to the minute with news and information they need to navigate their day.

The company's vision is to be the local leader for news, information and entertainment, with every household in Connecticut being served by a CT1 Media product every day.

Company evolution

Times Mirror purchased the Courant, which had been employee-owned, in 1979. Times Mirror merged with the Tribune Company in 2000.

FOX CT began in 1984 as a locally-owned, general entertainment station in competition with WCCT's predecessor, WTXX. Known as WTIC-TV at the time, the station became a charter Fox affiliate in 1986, while WCCT is affiliated with the CW Television Network. Over the years, FOX TV had several owners until it was sold to the Tribune Company, which subsequently purchased WTXX. Both stations became sister properties to the Courant in the Times Mirror and Tribune merger in 2000.

Fox TV's 10 o'clock newscast made its debut in 1989; weeknight 11 p.m. and weekday morning newscasts were added in 2008. Shortly after broadcasting its newscasts in high definition, the station added weekend morning and 4 p.m. newscasts, increasing the station's weekly local news output to the most of any station in the Hartford/New Haven market.

FOX CT began broadcasting in the Courant's newsroom in December 2009. The high-definition studio is one of the most technologically forward newsrooms in the country.

The Advocate Weekly Newspapers were linked to the Courant even before the newspaper bought the weeklies in 1999. Geoffrey Robinson and Edward Matys founded the company in 1973 while copy editors at the Courant. In 1973 they introduced the Hartford Advocate and the Valley Advocate, based in Amherst, Mass. The New Haven Advocate and the Fairfield County Advocate followed in 1975 and 1978, respectively. The Advocate weeklies offer an alternative viewpoint and a focus on entertainment.

Children cool off in the swimming pool at Camp Courant.

Camp Courant

The Courant and CT1 Media continue to support Hartford's Camp Courant, which began as a summer excursion fund in 1894 providing free summer activities for city children.

Camp Courant is the only summer camp serving Hartford youth that provides transportation, preventive and acute health and social work services, two nutritious daily meals and recreation, education and cultural activities at no cost to the camper or his or her family.

The 36-acre camp is one of the largest and oldest free day camps in the country providing enriching experiences for children ages 5 through 12 such as sports, swimming, arts and crafts, computer learning, yoga, financial literacy and photography.

Camp Courant believes that just because children are out of school during the summer does not mean children should stop learning. Children who participate in summer day camp programs often increase their self-perception and social skills. Research also shows that students who attended summer camp, either residential or day, improve their critical thinking, problem-solving and decision-making abilities. Providing children with quality, affordable, accessible care and enrichment, tutoring and recreation, is one of the most effective ways to prevent them from failing or dropping out of school, becoming teenage parents, or becoming involved in destructive behaviors. Camp Courant provides these positive activities for Hartford's most at-risk children.

Camp Courant typically serves between 400 to 600 children each day for six weeks. Campers learn to develop into healthy, responsible adults.

Over the years, broad-based community support has resulted in the expansion of programs and services to the children. All of the services are free, due to support from corporations, foundations, individuals, community groups and government grants. In-kind support provided by CT1 Media and other organizations helps keep administrative costs to a minimum, resulting in more services being available for more children.

Camp Courant is committed to these campers and to creating headline-worthy, picture-perfect summers to remember.

With its storied past, award-winning reporting and solid, multimedia news foundation on which to build, CT1 Media is more than equipped to meet today's demands and tomorrow's challenges. CT1 Media has been a welcome guest in Connecticut households for decades through its newspapers and newscasts. The media group will continue to bring community stories that educate and entertain its audiences whenever and however they want it — on phones, tablets, computers and through Facebook, Twitter or tomorrow's social media offerings.

"CT1 Media is a team focused on growth," Graziano says. "A team that views change as an opportunity."

AHLSTROM

Ahlstrom is a high performance materials company, partnering with leading businesses around the world to help them stay ahead.

Up until 2000, Windsor Locks, Connecticut, was home to the oldest corporation listed on the New York Stock Exchange, Dexter Corporation C.H. Dexter and Sons was established in 1767 — nine years before the American Revolution — as a small, family-owned sawmill that evolved into an international producer of specialty papers. Dexter focused its manufacturing around the aerospace, automotive, electronics, food packaging and medical markets.

Innovation and experimentation during the early 1900s led to the development of several new products that are still being produced today. In the 1930s, Dexter invented the Dexter wet forming long fiber nonwovens process. This process enabled the company to produce a new kind of filter material that was very light and porous, yet extremely strong. This invention provided the tea industry with the means to create a bag to strain tea leaves — what we now know as a teabag.

Around the same time, the long fiber process was used to develop some very promising applications such as fibrous meat casing, stencil base paper, and a general line of absorbent and filter papers. A few years later, Dexter devoted 100 percent of its production to long fiber papers and webs for industrial uses.

On its 200th birthday, Dexter publicly offered its shares and began to embark on a path of mergers and acquisitions that expanded the company's product offerings. In 2000 Dexter's nonwovens division — or paper division — was sold along with the company's original site in Windsor Locks. The buyer was Ahlstrom Corporation, a Finnish company ranked in the top ten of global manufacturers of nonwovens with facilities in the United States and Europe.

Today the Windsor Locks plant is one of Ahlstrom's largest manufacturing facilities, powered by roughly 450 employees. The plant produces nonwovens — fabric-like materials made from long fibers, bonded together by chemical, mechanical, heat or solvent treatments — for the medical, food, automotive, wall covering and specialty markets.

Since the acquisition, Ahlstrom has invested over $100 million in new process technology in Windsor Locks. Ahlstrom was seeking innovation and saw potential in Dexter. In 2001 the green light was given to build a composites manufacturing facility on site that would house the future of the nonwovens industry and Ahlstrom's next-generation composites.

Ahlstrom was listed on the Helsinki Stock Exchange in 2006. The company is now one of the world's leading producers of nonwovens, backed by its 32 product facilities and 28 sales offices worldwide. More than 5,000 employees serve customers in 26 countries on six continents and global product applications stretch across food and retail, medical and healthcare, building and utilities, transportation, household and consumer sectors.

Staying ahead

"We've come a long way because progress has always been our lifeblood. We need to ensure our customers stay ahead, too," said Jan Lång, Ahlstrom president and CEO. Ahlstrom has been building on its experience and know-how to anticipate customer needs for decades. Last year the company began making fundamental changes in its strategy, operating model and brand identity, strongly positioning Ahlstrom toward the future. Staying connected with what the market wants allows Ahlstrom to focus on its customers and create sustainable and profitable products and relationships.

Determined innovation led by outstanding sales and marketing teams is backed by a world-class supply chain and product development experts at Ahlstrom. Research and development and planning specialists keep the complex, diversified continuous process operations running on a 24/7 schedule, all supported by advanced information technology and finance divisions.

Ahlstrom's office building located at Two Elm Street in Windsor Locks.

Above: Ahlstrom manufactures nonwovens and specialty materials in the form of rolled goods. Left: The Windsor Locks plant was originally owned by C.H. Dexter & Sons dating back to 1767.

A sustainable future

Ahlstrom's strong dedication to sustainable development paves the way for better customer service, committed employees and green practices. For Ahlstrom, sustainability means a balance between economic, social and environmental responsibility.

Economic responsibility means responsible business conduct. Observing the laws of the host country, creating job opportunities, paying taxes and bringing prosperity to the region are all essential parts of the company's economic responsibility. Social responsibility is a natural part of Ahlstrom's way of operating. Safety is the most central value, but taking good care of employees — offering things like internal training — has always been a corporate priority. Environmental responsibility is minimizing the environmental impact of Ahlstrom's operations as much as possible, and it all starts at the beginning. More than 80 percent of the fibers Ahlstrom uses come from renewable resources.

The Ahlstrom way

Ahlstrom's values are the key principles that guide the company and the choices employees make every day. Employees respect each other and take care of the environment and the community around them, building trust. It's a company priority to link with customers, meet their needs and strive for excellence in customer service. And the company is always ready to change and evolve. Ahlstrom wants to learn and do things better. Employees share knowledge and development ideas both with the colleagues next to them and the ones working in other teams and units.

Act Responsibly.
Create Value.
Learn and Renew.

These three values help employees to act responsibly in situations where there is no guidance. The company's values are based on ways of working and who we are, supporting strategic direction and helping the company reach its goals.

Hartford Public Library

Hartford Public Library traces its roots back to 1774.

First known as the Library Company, it was started as a subscription company with some 700 books by a group of city leaders: Jonathan Brace, Jeremiah Wadsworth, Daniel Wadsworth, George Bull, Elisha Colt, Theodore Dwight, George Goodwin, Chauncey Goodrich and Thomas Y. Seymour. It continued to flourish into the early 1800s, but by the end of the century, Hartford residents recognized the need for a free public library. A request for funds went out to residents so that the Wadsworth Atheneum could be modified with a new library wing. More than 2,000 people donated money to the project, and within two years the city raised $406,000. On September 15, 1892, the new public library opened. On the first day, 388 names were registered and by the 10th day, 2,160 names. Then, on May 3, 1893, the library's name was formally changed to the Harford Public Library.

By World War II, the library had outgrown the Wadsworth Atheneum. It was time to build a modern library at a site at 500 Main Street. Since the library did not have the funds to finance new construction, the citizens of Hartford rose to the challenge and approved a 1951 bond issue for $2.7 million to make this dream come true. The 96,448-square-foot building, designed by Schutz & Goodwin, was completed in 1957. It was an architectural marvel of its time, built as a bridge over the Park River.

Less than 50 years later, the well-worn building was no longer able to serve the burgeoning needs of the City's residents. The library embarked on a 145,000-square-foot expansion and renovation of the downtown library, costing more than $42 million. Completed in 2007, a larger, more efficient library now serves the growing needs of the community. So as the city has grown, so has the library.

Throughout its rich history, the library has remained ahead of the curve. Caroline Hewins, the Hartford Public Library's first head librarian, led the library for 50 years, from 1875-1926. During her service, the number of volumes increased from 20,000 to 150,000. She also initiated the creation of the children's department in 1904, one of the first in the country. Hartford Public Library hired Dr. Spencer Shaw, one of Connecticut's first African-American librarians, in 1941. During the first half of the 20th century, nine branches were located throughout the City – the Dwight branch was the first in 1907 and the last branch, Blue Hills, in 1949. The Ropkins branch was relocated to shared space with the newly-constructed SAND school in 1998. In 2002, the Institute of Museum and Library Services awarded Hartford Public Library the National Service Award for Library Service. In 2010, the Library was honored for its commitment to the democratic humanity of the community by Librarians for Human Rights. In 2010 and 2011, Hartford Public Library was the only public library in the nation to receive federal grants for its work with New Americans from the United States Citizenship and Immigration Service. The historic Mark Twain branch was relocated to the historic Hartford Public High School in 2011 to provide broader services to our community's teenagers.

From the earliest days of the nation, the library has borne witness to a constantly changing and ethnically-diverse population. And as more immigrants and refugees arrived in Hartford, the library became the de facto immigration center, as well as a center for learning English, learning how to read, and developing job skills. "The Hartford Public Library has become a community gathering center for learning and exploring, for quality public education for all ages, for immigration and citizenship services, for job training and recreation," said Matthew K. Poland, the Library's chief executive officer and ninth leader of the institution since 1893.

The Hartford Public Library is known for its array of community-centered programs includ-

Hartford Public Library is a vital community technology hub for tens of thousands of residents because, for many, it is their only access to computers and the Internet.

ing the Teen Leader Program, a youth development program that prepares teens for the work place, and the Homework Club, which utilizes teen leaders to help students with their homework. For younger visitors, the library includes early education stations for children ages 3 through 9, that provide literacy games in Spanish and English, in addition to puzzles, play kitchen sets and state-of-the-art computers.

The library has had incredible success with its art and music programs. Hundreds of people gather every Sunday between January and May for the library's Baby Grand Jazz series. Residents are also encouraged to explore the library's ArtWalk, featuring works of artists who live and work in MetroHartford.

Hartford Public Library welcomes 860,000 visitors per year, seeking the staff's expertise. "There's something for every age group, from the very youngest to the oldest," Poland said.

Due to challenges in funding, rising operating expenditures and growing community demands, the library has diversified its revenue streams through grants and individual and corporate giving. For example, One Big Summer Night, the library's annual gala, is now one of the most anticipated events on Hartford's social calendar, raising nearly $150,000 in 2011. The gala has featured a noted author, an elegant reception, live and silent auctions and a summer supper, all to raise money for the library's literacy programs. Featured authors have included Wally Lamb, Julie Powell, and most recently Joe Scarborough and Mika Brzezinski, stars of MSNBC's Morning Joe.

Today the Library's online catalog and website make its holdings accessible to users wherever they are. The Library's collections themselves reflect the profoundly democratic and all-encompassing nature of the institution. Numbering more than a million, the library's collections range from venerable artifacts of our culture to popular materials that entertain and inform the everyday lives of a contemporary population.

All these things, taken together, make Hartford Public Library an irreplaceable and multifaceted institution. A useful way to understand the Library is to consider its beginnings and subsequent evolution. It has been very much a creature of time and place, bearing the imprint of its origins but always, like any living organism, coping with struggles and problems while adapting to an ever changing environment.

Top: A window into a place like no other, a world of opportunity.

Bottom: New Americans are drawn to the Library to learn English, to acclimate themselves and their families to the American culture, and to be embraced by their new community in Hartford.

Cigna

Grounded in centuries' old strong tradition of insurance, Bloomfield-based Cigna has become a leader in health services around the world.

The company traces its roots to 1792, when the Insurance Company of North America (INA) was founded in Philadelphia after meetings in Independence Hall. Nearly a century later, Connecticut General Life Insurance Company (CG) was founded in 1865 by Guy Phelps, M.D., a Simsbury native. Cigna, one of America's 10 oldest public companies, resulted from the merger of INA and CG in 1982.

Today Cigna is focused on a future of sustainable worldwide growth by dedicating itself to helping people improve their health, well-being and sense of security. The company operates in more than 30 countries and jurisdictions worldwide and has 66 million customer relationships.

Cigna's global headquarters in Bloomfield.

Consumers have long been passive about their health, reactive when they became sick, and virtually powerless when dealing with what is often a confusing and fragmented health care system. Today, however, people have a far greater interest in being involved. They actively seek health information, counseling about wellness and care and want to make choices based on quality and cost. In other words, they desire to be in control. As a result, much of the traditional insurance benefits — such as basic claims processing and contracting with health care professionals — are now considered simply the price of entry. Cigna is looking to go far beyond simply managing "sick care."

Led by President and Chief Executive David M. Cordani, Cigna has embraced a global strategy for growth entitled "Go Global, Go Deep and Go Individual" and launched a new Go You brand in 2011 — an innovative approach to meeting the evolving health and well-being needs of consumers. Cigna's Go You approach is all about leveraging the company's 33,000 global employees to support and nurture the unique strengths of every one its customers — so that each and every individual can reach their full potential.

To that end, Cigna supports its customers worldwide with 24/7/365 access in 150 languages, and health consultation and coaching. Cigna doctors, nurses, pharmacists, clinicians, health coaches and service teams work to engage and empower each customer through the media of their choice: online, on the phone, through mobile devices, and Facebook and Twitter. And the company works closely with one million health care professionals to ensure its customers have access to affordable, high quality health care.

The company's integrated suite of health, pharmacy, behavioral, dental, disability, life, accident and international products and services are offered to public, private and union customers around the world. As a result, Cigna continues to thrive in a dynamic and challenging environment. With 2010 revenue of $21.3 billion, Cigna is 122 on the Fortune 500 list of largest U.S. corporations.

Cigna's mission extends to the communities it serves locally, nationally, and across the globe: promoting wellness, expanding access to health information and services, developing leaders and encouraging collaborative, sustainable problem-solving approaches. Local initiatives include lead sponsorship of the National Champion UConn Men's Basketball Coach Jim Calhoun Cancer Challenge Ride and Walk in Simsbury. Nationally, Cigna is a lead sponsor of the March of Dimes® March for Babies℠, the United Way, the Juvenile Diabetes Research Fund and the Martin Luther King, Jr. Memorial. Cigna's global efforts range from natural disaster relief to instituting a Global Giving Fund to augment and expand existing community efforts.

Through the Cigna Foundation, the company has awarded $8.8 million in grants to health, education and community organizations last year alone. But what the company gives back to the communities it serves goes far beyond this funding. Cigna employees are involved with their communities every day, on the job and off. Cigna encourages volunteerism worldwide by offering employees up to eight paid volunteer hours each year. In 2010 alone, employees contributed more than 23,000 hours through company-supported community service activities. In addition, the company's innovative Mobile Learning Lab provided health education services in nearly 100 cities across the U.S.

In today's challenging health care environment, whether supporting a cause or delivering solutions, Cigna is taking an active role in shaping the health care of the future. Cigna works with business leaders, health care professionals and legislators to develop, sustainable solutions that improve both health care quality and costs. For example, Cigna is accelerating the expansion of its Collaborative Accountable Care organizations, which provide everything from preventive services to managing life-long conditions like diabetes and heart disease, so that more customers can benefit from a coordinated approach to care that results in quality, greater choice and less cost.

Looking ahead, Cigna is well positioned for continued success — with a winning combination of capabilities and compassion and a unwavering focus on improving the health, well-being and security of the people and communities it serves.

Above: Cigna CEO David Cordani (center) fires up coworkers and their families at the 2011 March of Dimes March for Babies. Cigna has been a lead sponsor for 17 years, contributing more than $25 million for healthy moms and babies.

Below: Cigna and Dr. Mache Seibel, a.k.a. DocRock, team up to produce a music video teaching kids five steps they can take to avoid getting H1N1.

PHOTOGRAPHIC MOMENTS 135

MetroHartford Alliance

The **MetroHartford Alliance** is Hartford's Chamber of Commerce and the Hartford Region's Economic Development Leader.

Formed in 2001, the MetroHartford Alliance united the business expertise of Hartford's Chamber of Commerce (founded in 1799) and the economic development leadership of the MetroHartford Economic Growth Council to create the Region's leading business and economic development organization.

The Alliance brings together nearly 1,000 businesses, education and healthcare institutions, municipalities, non-profit organizations, and government leaders who are invested in the Hartford Region's future economic growth and its viability for robust business development. To that end, the Alliance supports pro-growth legislation, helps local companies expand, assists start-ups, encourages government investment in key infrastructure assets, develops programs for young professionals, and recruits companies from out of state to build a presence in the Region.

The mission of the MetroHartford Alliance is to compete aggressively and successfully for jobs, talent and capital for the Hartford Region and to ensure that the Hartford Region is a premier place for all people to live, work, play and raise a family.

For more information, visit www.metrohartford.com.

Strategic Partners:

- AEG LLC
- Ahlstrom Nonwovens LLC
- AI Engineers, Inc.
- Albemarle Equities, LLC/ Konover Commercial Corp.
- American Institute
- Andrew Associates
- Anthem Blue Cross/Blue Shield
- Archdiocese of Hartford
- Aspen Re America
- AT&T, Inc.
- Bingham McCutchen LLP
- BKM Total Office
- Blum Shapiro
- Bradley International Airport
- Canton Chamber of Commerce
- Capital Community College
- CCR, LLP
- Central Connecticut State University
- CGI, Inc.
- Charter Oak State College
- Citizens Bank
- Cognizant Technology Solutions
- Comcast
- ConnectiCare, Inc. & Affiliates
- Connecticut Center for Advanced Technology
- Connecticut Community Investment Corporation
- Connecticut Natural Gas
- Connecticut Public Broadcasting Network
- Connecticut Science Center
- Day Pitney LLP
- Deloitte
- Dominion Resources Services, Inc.
- ebm-papst Inc.
- Ensign-Bickford Industries, Inc.
- Ernst & Young LLP
- Farmington Bank
- Farmington Chamber of Commerce
- FBE Limited LLC
- Filomeno & Company, P.C.
- First Niagara

MetroHartford Alliance Leadership Investors:

- The Hartford Financial Services Group
- The Travelers Companies, Inc.
- United Technologies Corporation
- Aetna Inc.
- CT1 Media Fox 61 The Hartford Courant
- Prudential Retirement
- UnitedHealthcare
- Hartford Hospital/Hartford HealthCare
- Saint Francis Hospital and Medical Center
- Northeast Utilities
- The Metropolitan District Commission
- The Phoenix Companies, Inc.
- Bank of America
- Webster Bank
- Connecticut Children's Medical Center

Left: Chuck Shivery, Chairman, President and Chief Executive Officer, Northeast Utilities is Chairman of the MetroHartford Alliance Board of Directors.
Right: The Alliance holds many events during the year where members can come together to network and grow professionally.

FirstLight Power Resources
Foxwoods Resort Casino
Goodwin College
Greater Hartford Arts Council
Griffin Land
Hartford Business Journal
HinckleyAllenSnyder LLP
Hoffman Auto Group
Horton International, LLC
Hospital for Special Care
ING U.S. Financial Services
Insurity, A LexisNexis Company
J. H. Cohn LLP
Kostin, Ruffkess & Co., LLC
KPMG LLP
LAZ Parking Ltd.
LEGO Systems, Inc.
Lincoln Educational Services
Lincoln Financial Group
Lux Bond & Green
Marchese Consulting LLC
MassMutual Financial Group
May, Bonee & Walsh, Inc.
McCarter & English, LLP
MetLife
Mintz & Hoke Inc.
Murtha Cullina LLP
OAKLEAF
Olsen Construction Services, LLC
Ovation
PCC Technology Group, LLC
People's United Bank
Pfizer Global Research & Development
Pita Group
PricewaterhouseCoopers, LLP
Pullman & Comley, LLC
Qualidigm
Reid and Riege, P.C.
Rensselaer Polytechnic Institute
Retail Brand Alliance, Inc. 
Robinson & Cole LLP
S/L/A/M Collaborative
Saint Francis HealthCare Partners
Saint Joseph College
Shipman & Goodwin LLP
Simsbury Chamber of Commerce
Sovereign/Santander Bank
St. Germain Investment Management
Stackpole, Moore, Tryon Tuesdays
Stanley Works
Sullivan & LeShane Public Relations, Inc.
TD Bank
The Bushnell
The Hartford Club
The Hartford Steam Boiler Inspection & Insurance Co./Munich RE
The Pert Group
The Society Room of Hartford
The Whale
TicketNetwork
TopCoder
Trane Commercial Systems
Travelers Championship
Trinity College
Trumpf Inc.
United Way of Central and Northeastern Connecticut
University of Connecticut
University of Hartford
Vantis Life
Virtus Investment Partners, Inc.
Virtusa
Wadsworth Atheneum Museum of Art
Walker Systems Support, Inc.
Waterford Hotel Group
Wells Fargo Advisors
Wethersfield Chamber of Commerce
WFSB/TV3 Meredith Corporation
Wiggin and Dana, LLP
Windsor Chamber of Commerce
Women's Health USA
World Youth Peace Summit
WorldBusiness Capital, Inc.
XL Group plc
Zag Interactive

Regional Investors:

Co-Communications, Inc.
Connecticut State University System
Erland Construction
Event Resources Inc.
Fidelco Guide Dog Foundation  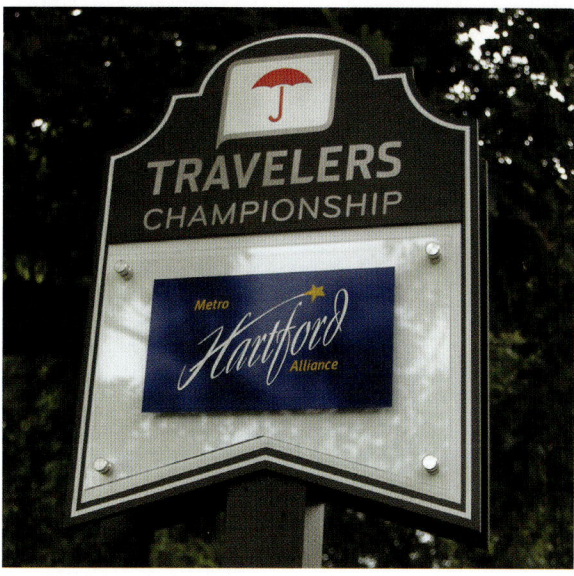
Fletcher-Thompson, Inc.
ForeSite Technologies
Fuss & O'Neill
Guilford Specialty Group, Inc.
Interscape Commercial Environments
JCJ Architecture
Marcum LLP
New England Financial Group, LLC
Post University
Purcell Associates
Sandler Training
The Perfect Promotion, LLC
We Work For Health - CT
Willis

Top Left: Oz Griebel, President and CEO of the MetroHartford Alliance, speaks at the Business Champions Awards Breakfast at the Connecticut Convention Center.

Top right: Members of HYPE (Hartford Young Professionals and Entrepreneurs) gather at the MetroHartford Alliance Annual Celebration. HYPE, which has nearly 4,000 members, is an initiative of the MetroHartford Alliance.

Bottom: The MetroHartford Alliance supports Hartford Region events, including sporting events. The Alliance is a founding sponsor of the Travelers Championship, the PGA TOUR event held annually in Cromwell, CT.

THE HARTFORD

The Hartford, founded in 1810, is a leading provider of insurance and wealth management services for millions of consumers and businesses.

Throughout its long history, The Hartford has insured some of the nation's most famous construction projects, including the Golden Gate Bridge and the Hoover Dam, and has paid claims related to some of the largest and most destructive disasters: the Great Chicago Fire of 1871, the San Francisco earthquake of 1906, and more recently, the September 11 terrorist attacks and Hurricane Katrina. Abraham Lincoln, Buffalo Bill Cody, Babe Ruth and Dwight Eisenhower are among the notable citizens who have been Hartford policyholders.

Today, The Hartford is a Fortune 100 company energized with a new vision for the future. In September 2009, the company welcomed Liam E. McGee as its chairman, president and chief executive officer.

Six months after his arrival, McGee announced his plans to organize The Hartford's operations around three businesses: commercial markets, wealth management and consumer markets. "We are organized around our key customer growth opportunities: risk protection and benefits for businesses, wealth management, and consumer risk protection for affinity groups and select customer segments," said McGee.

On May 10, 2010, The Hartford celebrated its 200th anniversary by ringing the bell at the New York Stock Exchange, sponsoring employee community service projects and events around the country, and recognizing agents and partners with philanthropic contributions in their honor. "For 200 years, this iconic American company has helped its customers achieve financial confidence, earning a reputation for trust, integrity and customer service excellence," McGee said as the company ushered in its third century. "We are well-positioned to move forward and have everything we need for success."

Integrity is the backbone of The Hartford's corporate culture and its reputation for honesty in business dealings is legendary. The company's commitment to ethical behavior continues to this day. The Ethisphere

Above: Speaking at West Middle Elementary School, The Hartford's CEO Liam McGee announces a $7 million commitment to support projects in the Asylum Hill neighborhood.

Right: The Hartford celebrates its bicentennial by ringing the opening bell of the NYSE on May 10, 2010.

Institute, a leading international think-tank dedicated to the creation, advancement and sharing of best practices in business ethics, has recognized The Hartford as one of the World's Most Ethical Companies for the last four consecutive years.

The Hartford has a long history of supporting the city from which it takes its name. More than a third of The Hartford's workforce is located in the Greater Hartford area and the company is deeply committed to making a positive impact right in its own backyard. For 90 years, the Asylum Hill neighborhood downtown has been home to The Hartford. The company has committed to invest $7 million to revitalize the neighborhood, improve education, bolster community support services and promote public safety and home ownership. "We want to make a difference for the families that live here, the children who study and play here and for the people who work here," said McGee. The Hartford is equally committed to reaching out with a helping hand to support other local, national and international communities. One of the company's major initiatives is its sponsorship of the U.S. Paralympics, demonstrating its belief that individuals can lead active, productive lives after a disabling event.

The Hartford is also committed to sustainable business practices. The company has been insuring renewable energy risks, including solar, wind and geothermal, for more than 20 years. In 2011, The Hartford installed electric-vehicle charging stations at its Hartford, Simsbury and Windsor offices and expanded insurance coverage to include home-based electric-vehicle chargers. "[It] demonstrates our support for developing the electric vehicle market and our commitment to a cleaner environment," said McGee.

The Hartford's logo captures the essence of what The Hartford stands for today – the stag stands tall and looks forward, linking The Hartford's heritage with a renewed sense of confidence, optimism and vitality. Two hundred years of experience have made The Hartford strong, but its focus is on the future and providing financial confidence to its 18 million customers. They can be confident that The Hartford is behind them as they work to achieve their goals.

Above: View of The Hartford's headquarters on Asylum Avenue.

Below: Employees from The Hartford participate in a Day of Caring to support the 2011 United Way campaign.

STANLEY BLACK & DECKER

Stanley Black & Decker — A Local Company with Global Resources.

In 1843, a man by the name of Frederick Stanley opened a small shop in New Britain, Connecticut to manufacture bolts, hinges, and other hardware from wrought iron. In 1857, Stanley's cousin, Henry Stanley, founded another shop in New Britain, the Stanley Rule and Level Company, which produced high quality hand tools.

In the early 1900s, the two companies merged to form The Stanley Works.

Right about the same time, in 1910, two men named S. Duncan Black and Alonzo G. Decker started a shop of their own in Baltimore, Maryland. Within six years the two men had obtained the world's first patent for a portable power tool. That patent would change the world of power tools, and make Black & Decker one of the most recognized names in the world.

In fact, both companies quickly built reputations for excellence and innovation, and built the Stanley and Black & Decker names into trusted and respected brands. Both companies flourished over the next 100 years, amassing an unparalleled family of brands and products and an even more impressive wealth of industry expertise.

In 2010, the two companies combined to form Stanley Black & Decker, the world's biggest and best tools and security company. While the two companies had grown in parallel, there was very little overlap between their operations, and the business units, product lines, and geographic locations complemented each other well. Combined as one Fortune 500 powerhouse, the company's portfolio features a host of respected brands including Stanley, Black & Decker, Bostitch, Porter-Cable, DeWalt, Sonitrol, Emhart Teknologies and dozens more, forming the foundation of the company's three major divisions: Construction and DIY, Industrial, and Security.

Construction and DIY

The largest and most established of Stanley Black & Decker's business units, Construction and DIY (Do-It-Yourself) delivers the hand tools and power tools that build, improve and repair our world. Hammers, drills, wrenches, tape measures, levels, flashlights — even a nail that can make a home twice as resistant to hurricanes and earthquakes — are all Stanley Black & Decker's stock in trade. Never complacent, the company has a rigorous product innovation methodology. With a laser focus on residential construction, repair and remodeling, Stanley Black & Decker's approach to new product development incorporates field-testing of new prototypes. Stanley's Discovery Teams integrates feedback from end-users into product designs to ensure maximum utility and customer satisfaction. An example is the DeWalt line of cordless compact lithium-ion power tools, launched in 2010 with more in the pipeline for future releases. The advantage of this technology is that batteries are smaller in size and lighter in weight than traditional Nickel-Cadmium batteries. The batteries do not self-discharge, allowing the tools to be stored for extended periods of time without losing charge. For any professional or do-it-yourselfer that has reached for a rechargeable electric screwdriver only to find it dead, the benefits and convenience are clear. Stanley has a well-earned reputation for delivering tough, innovative and trusted hand and power tools and storage solutions for both construction professionals and the do-it-yourselfers who want to work like pros.

Industrial

Stanley Black & Decker's expertise in tools extends far beyond residential building and remodeling into specialized areas such as industrial and automotive repair, engineered fastening systems and infrastructure solutions. These three business units form Stanley Black & Decker's Industrial division, and also includes some of the world's toughest tools for the world's

Above right: The steam-powered yard engine was purchased by the Stanley brothers in 1830. The engine was used only for short hauling between buildings. It was the first in New Britain and possibly in Connecticut.

Above: Frederick T. Stanley established Stanley's Bolt Manufacturing in 1843 and incorporated the Stanley Works in 1852.

toughest jobs. The range of industries and professions that use the company's tools and expertise is extensive — from auto mechanics and utility workers to hi-tech professionals assembling and repairing biomedical devices and military aviation controls. To meet the large-scale storage needs of the industries it serves, Stanley Black & Decker provides solutions for military and heavy equipment, auto dealers, manufacturers, agriculture — and even the Smithsonian Institution, to safeguard its large and eclectic collection of historical and archival material.

Emhart Teknologies, based in Shelton, CT, forms the core of Stanley's engineered fastening systems business. Emhart is an innovative powerhouse in manufacturing assembly technologies from concept through installation, capable of solving virtually any manufacturing challenge, anywhere in the world. At Emhart Teknologies, they emphasize the total system (the fastener, the installation tooling, and the assembly process), which ensures that customer productivity is maximized and the lowest possible cost is achieved. For some new customers an existing product such as a motor vehicle may be disassembled completely and analyzed for re-assembly in an entirely new and better way. Emhart engineers walk through existing assembly lines to devise better methods.

The need for infrastructure in the developing world is immense, with current levels of spending in the range of $1-2 trillion. Stanley hydraulic tools are widely used in emerging markets to construct roads, utilities, pipelines for oil, gas, water and sewers, airports, dams, bridges and tunnels, energy grids, railroads, ports and offshore platforms. Stanley's recent acquisition of CRC-Evans International extends the company's foothold in this lucrative market. CRC-Evans is a leading global supplier of specialized tools, equipment and services for the construction of oil and natural gas transmission pipelines.

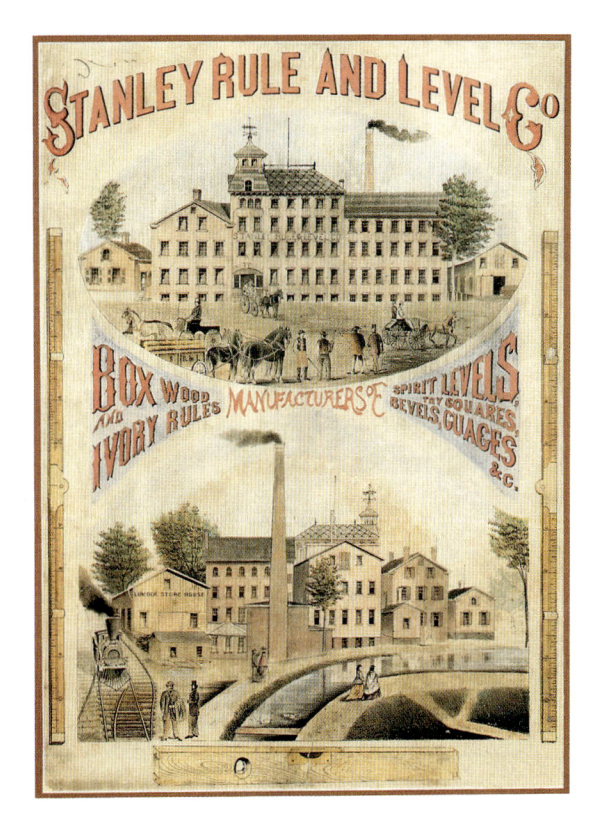

Security

If you've ever walked through an automatic door, chances are Stanley Black & Decker made it. A tour of your home will probably reveal other items manufactured by Stanley Security Solutions, from hinges and hooks to locks and keys. Today, as the world grows ever more security-conscious, Stanley Black & Decker is at the forefront, with solutions to meet the needs of consumers, government and industry.

From the simple to the sophisticated, whether mechanical or electronic, the company's products are widely used in industries as diverse as healthcare, education, banking, retail, transportation, automotive and infrastructure. A growing segment for Stanley Black & Decker is healthcare. Since 2002, the company has added solutions for resident safety, healthcare storage and patient security. The acquisition of InfoLogix in 2010 further expands Stanley Healthcare

Above: A broadside from the 1860s, reprinted in 1995 by John Walter.

Left: A photograph of the Stanley Rule & Level Company Sound Money Club, taken outside the company offices during William McKinley's successful 1896 presidential campaign.

Continued on next page

Continued from previous page

STANLEY BLACK & DECKER

Solutions' capabilities into mobility solutions, ensuring that critical information is available at the exact place and time it is needed. InfoLogix mobility solutions are in place in more than 1,400 hospitals in North America.

Security represents a significant growth opportunity for the company. Since 2002, the company has grown its Security Division from $200 million to more than $3 billion in revenues. With the acquisition of Swedish-based systems integrator Niscayah in September 2011 — the largest Security acquisition ever for the combined company — Stanley is poised to dramatically expand its convergent security growth platform and footprint. The acquisition demonstrates Stanley's continued pursuit of its stated strategic goals to continue expanding and developing its global security platform. Niscayah adds scale to the company's North American Security business and expands its presence into 12-plus European countries/regions where it did not have a security solutions presence.

The Key to Success: Stanley Fulfillment System

A major driver of the company's success is the Stanley Fulfillment System, or SFS. This concept captures a way of thinking, planning and doing business that is embraced by the entire organization. By adhering to the principles of SFS to improve working capital management, Stanley has freed up hundreds of million dollars of cash, enabling the company to both grow organically and aggressively pursue its acquisition strategies. "In 2007 our working capital turns were 4.5," said CEO Lundgren in his annual letter to shareholders. "Through the implementation of SFS principles over the succeeding three years, we were able to improve overall turns for legacy Stanley to 8.6 in 2010." The key components of SFS are: Sales & Operations Planning to balance supply and demand; Operational Lean to eliminate waste; Complexity Reduction to reduce cost while increasing speed of execution and customer satisfaction; Global Supply Management to leverage the company's scale; Order-to-Cash Excellence to provide a user-friendly customer purchasing experience; and Common Platforms to standardize business processes.

Innovation as the Lifeblood

As diverse as they may seem, each of Stanley's business units is similar in its passion for consistent and relentless innovation. Innovation is at the heart of the company's growth and vitality, and each business unit has instilled innovation deep into their new product development processes.

That's how the company can keep improving on tools it introduced to the world more than 100 years ago, and it's how the company can keep introducing brand new products that the world has never seen before. It's also how the company can ensure that a consistent portion of its revenue is derived from prod-

Above Right: A group of employees of Stanley Rule & Level Co.

Right: This dramatic photograph of two men suspended from the shaft of a Stanley Hammer was used in advertisements during the thirties to demonstrate the unusual strength of Stanley tools.

ucts that weren't on the shelves three years ago.

Passion is Palpable

In his closing comments to shareholders in 2010, CEO Lundgren paid tribute to the company's employees, viewing them as the company's #1 asset. Without their skill and dedication, Stanley's extraordinary performance would not be possible. "The most important part of our success derives from our people, whose passion for this Company, its customers and its future is palpable," said Lundgren. Stanley focuses on the continuous development of its people. With a large and ever increasing number of new ventures, products and markets, the needs are great and the opportunities for employees are abundant. Stanley employees are proud of their strong organization and its impressive achievements.

Giving Back

With the unshakeable belief that supporting the vitality of the communities it serves is critical to its success as a company, Stanley directly supports causes that are closely aligned to its business operations, and strives to make the world a better place. The company focuses on: affordable housing construction, reconstruction, and rehabilitation; technical, vocational, mathematics, science, and engineering education; hospitals and select healthcare-related charities; organizations with particularly compelling impact in areas where Stanley Black & Decker maintains a significant population of employees.

The company is a major supporter of Habitat for Humanity nationally and in the Hartford area, in particular. The company has partnered with Rebuilding Together New Britain, an organization dedicated to providing home repair and improvement services free of charge to low-income homeowners in need. Stanley employees are actively involved with these efforts, and Stanley also encourages employee giving with a 100% matching gifts program.

The future looks bright for Stanley Black & Decker. The company's success is no accident. It is the result of superior leadership, innovation and commitment to excellence honed over more than a hundred years. By staying close to the principles that got Stanley where it is today, this global diversified industrial giant will continue to be the standard bearer for corporate excellence for years to come.

DeWalt abrasives at work at a fabricator plant in Chicago, Illinois.

DeWalt power tools and Stanley FatMax® hand tools are the professional's choice.

Bedside charting carts from Stanley Healthcare secure medications and help enhance patient care.

Jacksonville International Airport (Jacksonville, Florida) relies on Dura-Glide 3000 Automated Entrances equipped with Stan-Vision™ sensors.

McCarter & English, LLP

Established in 1844, McCarter & English, LLP, is among the oldest and largest law firms in the United States.

Above: From left, McCarter & English, LLP attorneys John Mallin, Catherine Mohan, John Robinson, Pamela Moore, Charles Ray, and Eric Grondahl gather in the library of the firm's Hartford offices at CityPlace I.

First established in New Jersey, McCarter & English, LLP has offices in Boston, Hartford, Stamford, New York City, Newark, Philadelphia, and Wilmington. The firm arrived in Hartford in 2001 thanks to its office founder, Catherine Mohan, firm treasurer and member of the firm's executive committee.

The addition of the Hartford office reflected mutual industry commitments, as well as shared depth in intellectual property, business litigation, corporate, labor and employment, real estate, environmental, construction, and national toxic tort and product liability law. Drawing on McCarter & English's resources, track record, and offices throughout the Northeast Corridor, the Hartford office offers a deep platform of support for its clients. The firm's 400+ attorneys are known for their skill and strategic insights used to assist their clients with the business challenges that exist in core industry areas including Life Sciences, Technology, Financial Services, Consumer & Industrial Products, Real Estate and Construction. Today, McCarter & English's Hartford office has grown to 45 attorneys and is a key part of a nationally recognized law firm among Fortune 500 companies, midcap firms, and private businesses.

Key to McCarter & English's success is its commitment to understanding its clients' business objectives and answering their needs with high-quality and responsive services. "We listen closely to our clients' concerns and strive to be an advisor in the business sense, as much as in the legal sense," said Eric Grondahl, Hartford office managing partner.

In addition to its tradition of service to clients throughout the Northeast, McCarter & English remains actively committed to the civic and charitable organizations in its surrounding communities. One of the firm's most successful initiatives involves its work with the Connecticut Innocence Project, a division of the state's public defender's services that identifies individuals convicted of crimes of which they are innocent. McCarter & English provides office space for the organization's operation in Hartford, but the firm's real efforts for the cause are in the legal services provided pro bono. "We've partnered with them to review cases for individuals who may have been wrongly convicted of crimes," Grondahl said. "Particularly essential to the project, we continue our support for the people who are exonerated and released, and we help them get back into society."

The firm supports the rejuvenation efforts of downtown Hartford through its involvement with organizations like the Knox Park Foundation and Rebuilding Together. In addition, McCarter & English is a proud corporate sponsor of many community organizations like the Greater Hartford Arts Council, the Bushnell Center for Performing Arts, Community Partners in Action, Connecticut Fair Housing, and Greater Hartford Legal Aid.

McCarter & English's Hartford office is located on the 36th and 37th floors of CityPlace I. Visit the firm's website at www.mccarter.com.

PwC

> PwC has been a prominent member of the Hartford business community since the 1950s, first opening our doors to provide accounting services to local companies.

*M*ore than 60 years later, we remain steadfastly committed to Greater Hartford and supporting its people, businesses, schools, and civic/charitable organizations.

As the region's business environment has grown more diverse and complex over the years, our professional services and capabilities have broadened significantly. Today, PwC helps Hartford business executives create tailored solutions to meet the challenges and opportunities of doing business in the US and beyond. We focus on audit and assurance, tax, and advisory services, including human resources, deals, forensics, and consulting services. We serve clients across the industry spectrum and bring a global perspective, along with in depth knowledge of local, state, and national issues. Our reputation lies in building lasting relationships with our clients and delivering value in all that we do.

PwC is Hartford's leading professional services firm, with 30 partners and more than 350 staff members — nearly one-third of whom are CPAs. We provide audit services to more U.S. public companies headquartered in Hartford than all other firms combined.[1] Our professionals in the Hartford office are supported by a global network of approximately 140,000 people in 149 countries. With our highly skilled team of audit, tax, and advisory professionals, our clients benefit from our deep technical expertise and industry knowledge.

At PwC, our people are our biggest asset. We invest in many programs aimed at developing future leaders in the Hartford business community, both within our walls and in the broader marketplace. We focus our recruiting efforts on attracting top talent from Hartford-area schools and bring in both interns and new associates every year. Once these talented individuals are members of the PwC family, we commit to helping them succeed in their careers.

PwC is dedicated to making a difference where it matters most — right in our own backyard. Our culture of giving back is ingrained in everything that we do; we take our commitment to making Hartford a better place to live and work seriously. Our community efforts are focused on inspiring action, instilling pride, and nurturing economic stability in the Greater Hartford area. We support many local tax-exempt organizations and educational institutions throughout the year, and partners and staff give back to their communities by serving on boards of directors for not-for-profit organizations and participating in our annual Community Service Day — when more than 300 PwC employees volunteer across the Hartford region.

Since the 19th century, PwC has been helping companies navigate complex challenges and succeed in shifting economies. Looking ahead, we remain committed to providing that same high quality of client service and expanding our service capabilities. We look forward to continued investment in our clients, people, and the local community — delivering value to Greater Hartford in every way.

[1] Audit Analytics, Revenue (iDP, AA, 10k) July, 2011

PwC's Hartford partners and staff gather together.

AETNA

Aetna is one of the World's Most Admired Companies, according to Fortune Magazine.

Aetna is one of the World's Most Admired Companies, according to Fortune Magazine. The annual rankings to earn the title of Most Admired are based on multiple criteria, such as quality of management, financial soundness, long-term investment value and social responsibility to the community and the environment. Aetna has received countless awards that together paint a vibrant picture of its leadership in corporate America, including recognition for its business processes, technology innovations, sustainability initiatives and diversity programs.

Founded in 1853, Aetna is one of the nation's leading providers of health care, dental, pharmacy, group life, and disability insurance, and employee benefits. Aetna's expertise lies also in helping the international community address the challenge of access to affordable health care. The company's mission is to help people achieve health and financial security by providing easy access to safe, cost-effective, high-quality health care and protecting clients' finances against health-related risks. A Fortune 100 company, Aetna's annual revenues topped $34 billion in 2010, with 18.3 million medical members, 13.8 million dental members and 8.8 million pharmacy members.

Aetna has been guided by visionary leaders who understand that businesses benefit by taking a strong interest in the state of society as a whole. In 1959, then-chairman Henry S. Beers declared corporate social responsibility a key business objective for Aetna. The following year he made his case to the rest of corporate America in a still-famous speech to the American Management Association titled, "Responsibility of Business to Society." Beer's successor, Olcott D. Smith, further strengthened the company's commitment, creating Aetna's Corporate Social Responsibility Department in 1971. Today Aetna's corporate responsibility initiatives focus on five areas: community involvement, diversity, public policy leadership, environmental practices and corporate governance.

Community involvement and volunteerism have been hallmarks of Aetna's culture for 80 years. In 1931 the company launched its first employee United Way/Combined Health Charities Appeal to support the needs of the Hartford community. In 1972, Chairman John H. Filer, who many consider to be the father of corporate philanthropy, created the Aetna Foundation. "Few aspects of American society are more characteristically, more famously American than the nation's array of voluntary organizations, and the support in both time and money that is given to them by its citizens," said Filer. He strongly believed that corporations have an obligation to their communities, and believed both giving and volunteering to be vital to building and maintaining healthy communities. Throughout its history, the Aetna Foundation has strengthened disease prevention programs; revitalized neighborhoods; supported the arts, education and people in need; and championed diversity. Since 1980, Aetna and the Aetna Foundation have contrib-

Below: 2011 Hole in the Wall Camp Challenge Ride Aetna.

Aetna headquarters, located in Hartford.

uted $394 million in grants and sponsorships. Aetna's legacy of community involvement and volunteerism is part of its past, its present and its future. "As a corporate citizen, Aetna has certain responsibilities," said Mark Bertolini, Aetna's chairman, CEO and president. "Our company's leaders and our actions can set an example for others."

Today, the Aetna Foundation is emerging as a forward-thinking national health foundation focused on improving population health in three key ways: improving racial and ethnic equity in the health care system, curtailing the obesity epidemic that threatens the health of so many Americans, including our children, and building a more integrated health care system that delivers improved quality of care more efficiently and effectively. Working with leading institutions such as the Brookings Institution, the Institutes of Medicine, AcademyHealth, and Health 2.0, as well as numerous universities, the Aetna Foundation is helping to establish the science, the data, and the proof behind new solutions to these vexing problems to help inform public policy and drive lasting change and improvement.

At the same time, Aetna is working and giving locally — in Connecticut and across the nation — to improve the communities where its customers and employees live and work. Aetna understands that healthy, vibrant people and healthy, vibrant communities go hand in hand, so across our markets we consider grant-making opportunities that will have a wide-ranging and positive impact on the public health, the local economy and the social programs that support each community.

The Aetna Employees Reaching Out (AERO) is the vehicle through which the company's 33,000 employees are empowered, motivated and mobilized to be a force for good in their own communities across the country. In 2003, Aetna celebrated its 150th anniversary, and launched to build on employees' enthusiasm for volunteerism. Last year Aetna employees generously donated nearly 335,000 hours of their personal time and talents; Connecticut volunteer hours represented almost 30 percent of the total. During the same period, Aetna and the Aetna Foundation awarded $15.6 million in grants to 661 nonprofits and employees gave additional financial

Continued on next page

Continued from previous page

AETNA

support totaling $6.9 million to 9,942 organizations nationwide. Since 2003, employees have logged more than 2.3 million volunteer hours. Today there are 50 regional volunteer councils that identify local community needs and respond accordingly. Connecticut is home to two councils, one in Hartford and the other in Norwalk.

Aetna generously supports the efforts of employees who wish to engage in philanthropic endeavors of their own. The company offers matching grants for disaster response and personal donations; matches donations to the annual Giving Campaign; offers volunteer grants to organizations where employees donate their time; and allows employees to take time off to volunteer through its Volunteer Hours program without having to use vacation time. Many Aetna employee heroes have emerged as a result of Aetna's corporate commitment to service. For example, consider the work of two Aetna employees:

Above: Cheryl Nelson, an Aetna senior customer service representative.

Right: How Does Your Garden Grow? – Kids from Hartford's low-income neighborhoods had the opportunity to plant, cultivate, and harvest their own food at a community garden with help from Aetna employees, who supplied seeds, tools, know-how, and encouragement throughout the summer.

Cheryl Nelson, an Aetna senior customer service representative in Bismarck, North Dakota, participated in a bone-marrow donation drive run by the Be The Match(SM) Foundation. The Aetna Foundation and Aetna have awarded more than $160,000 over several years to this foundation, and most of the grants have been used add Aetna employees to the National Marrow Donor registry. Adding one person to the registry costs about $100. When Nelson found out she was a match for a leukemia patient, she was thrilled. "It felt like I had won the lottery, except I won an once-in-a-lifetime opportunity to give someone a second chance at life," she said. Nelson underwent blood testing and a health assessment. In the fall of 2009, she traveled some 1,500 miles to donate her marrow.

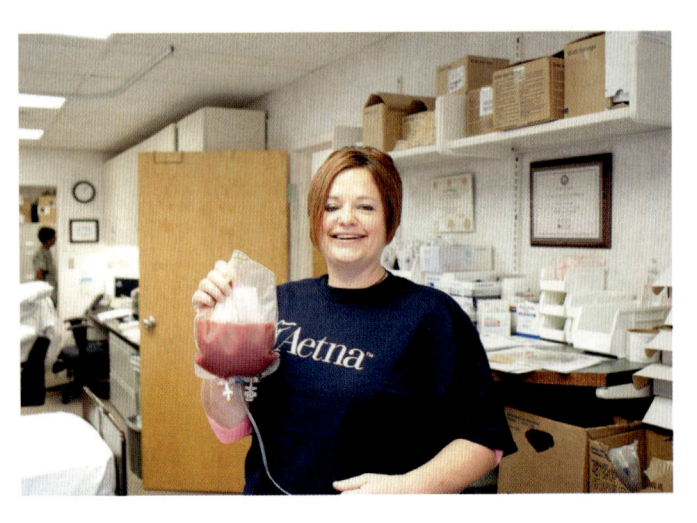

Over the years, Lisa Smith's hard work and dedication has helped an inner-city hot meals program in Akron, Ohio grow to serve an average of 220 people at dinner four to five times a month. Smith, an Aetna Service Operations teleworker, oversees other volunteers who prepare and serve meals. She also has helped the organization with capacity-building efforts through grant writing, although she had no previous fundraising experience. "We're getting a three-door refrigerator soon, replacing one that is at least 35 years old," Smith said, showing that her hard work learning how to apply for grants has paid off. Smith has a simple piece of advice for people thinking about volunteering. "Go out and do it," she said. "You'll be so glad you did. What I've gotten back is so much more than I've given."

Throughout its history, Aetna has built deep and lasting relationships in Hartford, Connecticut, where Aetna is headquartered and where the company maintains a large presence, of over 6,000 employees.

Aetna and the Aetna Foundation, as well as generations of employees, have supported a wide range of charitable organizations, primarily in Hartford, representing health issues, the arts, social services such as food, shelter and clothing for those in need, academic studies, faith-based programs and many other worthwhile initiatives. In recent years, our annual gifts in greater Hartford have typically ranged between $5 million and $7 million each year.

In 2010, Aetna announced a three-year, $750,000 commitment to help save a premier tennis tournament played each summer in Connecticut. As a

Cornerstone Partner in the reinvigorated New Haven Open at Yale, Aetna is focused on activities that will engage the whole family in the excitement of the tournament and the health and vitality that come with physical activity such as tennis. Aetna also announced a three-year, $500,000 commitment to professional hockey in Hartford. As the first member of the Whaler's Alliance, is the title sponsor of the Connecticut Whale's new Amateur Hockey program.

Aetna also has provided long term support for the Go Red for Women movement in Connecticut, which is part of a national effort by the American Heart Association to inform, empower and rally women to stop cardiovascular disease, the No. 1 cause of death among women. Each year the disease claims the lives of 500,000 women. Go Red for Women offers educational programs, advancing women's understanding about their risk for heart disease and providing tools and motivation to help women reduce their risk.

Aetna has also been a multi-year sponsor of Paul Newman's Hole in the Wall camps. These camps serve more than 44,000 children with cancer, HIV/AIDS, diabetes, asthma, hemophilia, and other serious illnesses by enabling them to enjoy an empowering outdoor recreational summer camp experience free of charge. An initial grant in 2009 of $50,000 launched the Hole in the Wall Camp Challenge Ride, raising $215,000 for the original Hole in the Wall Gang camp in Ashford, Connecticut. Based on its success, Aetna expanded the grant the following year to $250,000 to support rides benefiting the Ashford camp as well as two other Hole in the Wall camps in New York and California. Aetna's Volunteer Councils helped to develop and manage regional Team Hole in the Wall Camp Challenge Rides. In 2011, Aetna committed another $210,000 for a total of five rides across the country with the expectation that in total these events will raise up to half a million dollars for the camps across the country. In addition to supporting the rides, many Aetna volunteers participate in volunteer days and team marathon events, craft no-sew blankets for campers and support the overall needs of the camps.

Aetna and the Aetna Foundation have given substantial support to the arts and cultural life of its hometown. "Arts affect our bodies," says Kate Bolduc, CEO of the Greater Hartford Arts Council. "A 2009 study found that by simply listening to music, you could decrease your blood pressure, lower your heart rate, and ease anxiety." Aetna is the named sponsor of the Greater Hartford Arts Council's Aetna First Thursdays, featuring a variety of music, theater, exhibitions and other cultural events. Through its funding of the Greater Hartford Arts Council, Aetna is able to offer financial support to numerous arts institutions and programs across Hartford, including TheaterWorks, The Hartford Stage, The Bushnell, the Wadsworth Atheneum and other institutions.

The ripple effect of these actions is far-reaching, influencing 33,000 employees, the nearly 10,000 nonprofit organizations they support, and ultimately, the individuals whose lives are enriched by Aetna's Culture of Caring and its efforts to make the world a better place. "We're in the business of helping people live full and healthy lives, and embracing our corporate citizenship is fundamental to our ability to fulfill that mission," said former chairman and CEO Ronald A. Williams in Aetna's 2010 corporate responsibility report.

The Holiday Spirit – Aetna Chairman, CEO and President Mark Bertolini and employee Denise Zachmann celebrate the generosity of Aetna employees, surrounded by more than 600 gaily wrapped packages of toys, warm clothing, household goods and gift cards for people in need that were purchased by employees through the annual giving tree program. The Aetna Foundation also presented surprise $2,000 holiday grants to the 13 nonprofit partners that identified the families to receive the gifts to help the organizations better serve their clients.

Hartford Hospital

Hartford Hospital is a special place, a destination medical center.

Hartford Hospital has an impressive history and deep roots in the community. It was founded in 1854 after an explosion at the Fales and Gray Car Factory injured dozens of workers, many of them critically. At the time, there was no central place to care for the injured. But that would soon change. The accident would galvanize the community, paving the way for Hartford Hospital, the first general acute care hospital to be built in the area.

More than 150 years later, Hartford Hospital has built on that rich history and solid foundation. It is

The front entrance of Hartford Hospital, founded in 1854.

now one of the largest teaching hospitals and tertiary care centers in all of New England, with more top-ranked physicians than any other area hospital. Hartford Hospital is at the center of robust clinical research, funded by annual grants of more than $14 million. Of the 19 hospitals in the Hartford, Connecticut metropolitan area, Hartford Hospital was ranked #1 in U.S. News & Word Report's latest regional ranking. Hartford Hospital's long term care facility, Jefferson House, has been providing services for seniors since 1873.

It was Hartford Hospital that brought robotic surgery to Connecticut. Years later, the hospital has become New England's second busiest surgical practice, second only to Mass General in Boston. Expert physicians perform more minimally invasive surgery than any other hospital in the region.

Hartford Hospital houses the area's only Level 1 Trauma Center. It owns and operates LIFE STAR, the state's critical care helicopter service which has been saving lives since 1985. In those years, the LIFE STAR team has transported more than 20,000 patients.

Hartford Hospital has always been at the cutting edge of medicine. The teaching hospital has trained the next generation of doctors for more than 150 years. In those years, medical education has changed dramatically, and Hartford Hospital has been at the forefront, creating the area's first Center for Education, Simulation and Innovation (CESI). At CESI, health care workers come from across the state and beyond to learn how to help and heal patients. CESI allows first responders to practice under simulated, real-world circumstances, so they will be better prepared when a real emergency call comes.

Hartford Hospital is a vital member of the state's only true integrated health system, Hartford HealthCare, which provides comprehensive, coordinated and compassionate care throughout a patient's lifetime.

Hartford Hospital is a special place, a destination medical center that is ingrained in its local community. And while it has an amazing past, the future is even more exciting. Hartford Hospital is leading the charge, becoming a model for health care of the future.

Hartford Hospital's major centers of excellence include:

The Helen & Harry Gray Cancer Center

The Helen & Harry Gray Cancer Center is a nationally-recognized cancer center and one of the largest, most comprehensive in the Northeast. It is one of two facilities in New England appointed by the National Cancer Institute as a participant in the NCI Community Cancer Centers Program. The Helen & Harry Gray Cancer Center offers the latest technology to provide cutting edge, state-of-the-art care and is home to many talented and experienced medical specialists.

The Henry Low Heart Center

The Henry Low Heart Center provides the region's

best cardiac health options. It is dedicated to the care of the heart and all its complexities. It offers outstanding multi-disciplinary cardiovascular programs designed to provide excellence in treatment, diagnosis and management through the entire spectrum of cardiovascular disease. The center is named for Dr. Henry Low, a pioneering cardiac surgeon who performed the first successful heart transplant operation in Connecticut in 1984.

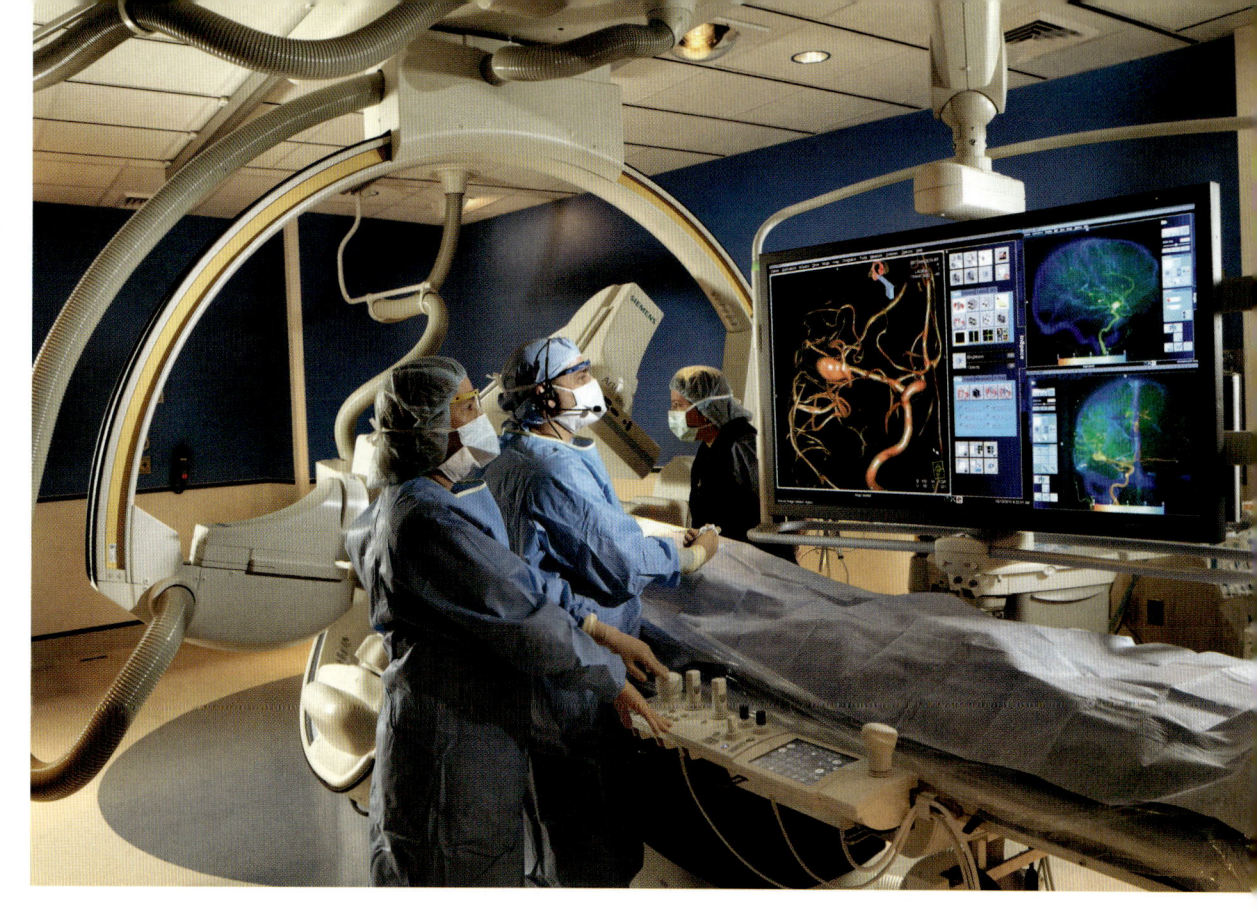

Robotic and Minimally Invasive Surgery

The team at Hartford Hospital has more experience in robotic and minimally invasive surgery than any other hospital in the region. Hartford Hospital originated techniques that are now used worldwide. Patients benefit from reduced bleeding, less pain, smaller risk of internal scarring, a shorter hospital stay and a shorter recovery.

Neurosciences

Hartford Hospital is a leader of neurological care in the region, recognizing the complexities and challenges of treating brain and spine-related diseases and injuries. Hartford Hospital brings together expert physicians, state-of-the-art technology, cutting-edge treatment options, and superior patient-oriented care to deliver the best possible outcomes. Hartford Hospital is one of the only hospitals in the region offering cutting edge options like awake brain surgery and tumor removal through the nose.

The Stroke Center

The Stroke Center celebrated its 10th anniversary in 2011, and has become the most comprehensive stroke clinic in the area with specialized care available 24 hours a day, seven days a week. Hartford Hospital's Stroke Center is a regional leader in patient care, education and clinical research, and was the first Primary Stroke Center certified by the Joint Commission in the entire New England region. The program received the Gold Plus Achievement Award in 2010 and 2011 from the American Heart Association/American Stroke Association. In 2011, the Center created its first Patient Advisory Board to improve the patient experience within the Hartford HealthCare system.

The Spine Center

Hartford Hospital performs more inpatient spinal procedures than any other hospital in the state. The Spine Center offers unmatched experience and skill, with a variety of specialists who can perform the diagnosis, treatments or procedures patients need to get back on their feet. Surgeons at Hartford Hospital also have the O-arm® Surgical Imaging System which provides spinal surgeons with GPS precision during procedures. This means less invasive surgery, shorter recuperation time for patients and increased confidence in their physicians.

Above: Dr. Gary Spiegel examines images in one of the neuroradiology biplane labs at Hartford Hospital. The biplane lab includes a state-of-the-art imaging system that gives doctors a three-dimensional view of blood vessels in the brain, enabling them to repair aneurysms, perform therapeutic procedures and correct vessel blockages such as a stroke.

Left: LIFE STAR enroute to a life-saving call. Hartford Hospital owns and operates LIFE STAR, the state's only air ambulance system.

Continued on next page

Continued from previous page

HARTFORD HOSPITAL

The Institute of Living

The Institute of Living is Hartford Hospital's Division of Psychiatry. The Institute was one of the first mental health centers in the United States — and the first hospital of any kind in Connecticut. Today, it is a leader in patient care, research and education in the fields of behavioral, psychiatric and addiction disorders. The Institute was named one of the top-ranked psychiatric facilities in the nation by U.S. News & World Report in 2007, 2008 and 2009, and was the first in Connecticut to offer transcranial magnetic stimulation therapy for the treatment of depression.

The Transplant Program

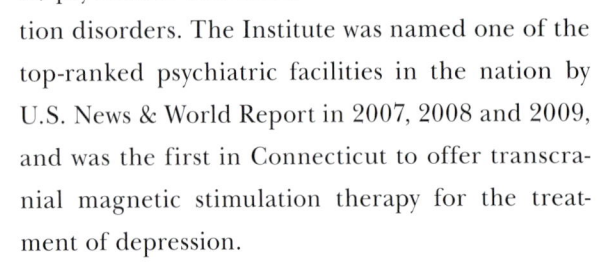

Hartford Hospital is one of only two transplant centers in Connecticut and the only hospital in the state offering ventricular assist device destination therapy, another option for patients with advanced heart failure. Hartford Hospital's first kidney transplant was performed on March 25, 1971. As the technology and science of transplantation advanced, the hospital added liver and heart transplantation in 1984. New initiatives are constantly underway. Some of these include expanding the living donor pool, cryosurgery and associated technologies for liver cancer. The Transplant Program is certified by the United Network for Organ Sharing.

Women's Health Services

Hartford Hospital is committed to the comprehensive health care of women, at every stage of a woman's life to ensure the best possible care, ranging from routine wellness to the very latest treatments for high-risk pregnancies, pelvic floor disorders and gynecologic cancers. Hartford Hospital physicians are leaders in national medical societies and serve on the faculties of medical schools at Dartmouth and the University of Connecticut.

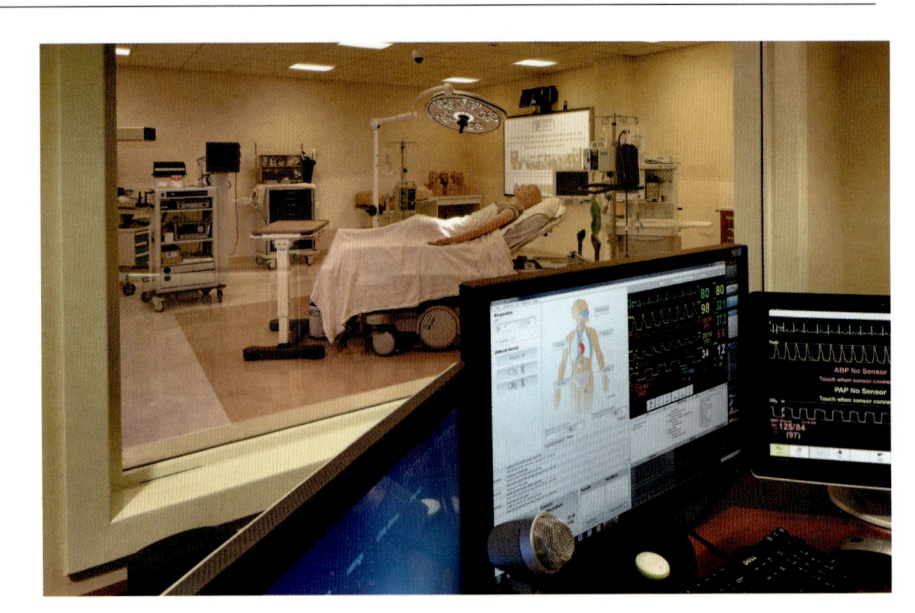

The Joint Center

The Total Joint Center is a regional leader in joint replacement and helps thousands of patients get their lives back on track. Hartford Hospital's experienced team provides excellent care as part of a comprehensive program that also includes patient education and post-operative physical therapy.

The Surgical Weight Loss Center

The Surgical Weight Loss Center at Hartford Hospital is the only hospital in Connecticut to be designated a Bariatric Surgery Center of Excellence by both the American Society of Metabolic and Bariatric Surgery and the American College of Surgeons. Because every patient is unique, the Hartford Hospital team customizes a care plan for every individual with multiple resources and services.

Gastroenterology

From routine screenings and common tests to advanced procedures and complex cases, Hartford Hospital's Gastroenterology Division offers the expert diagnostic and treatment capabilities that referring physicians demand, combined with the compassionate care every patient deserves.

Colorectal Surgery

There has been a revolution in the past 15 years in colorectal surgery and Hartford Hospital surgeons have led the charge. Operations that used to require lengthy, open incisions can now be performed using just a three-inch incision, plus tiny openings for a camera and instruments.

A glimpse inside the control room at Hartford Hospital's Center for Education, Simulation and Innovation, where life-like, fully responsive computerized replicas of the human body allow medical students, practicing doctors, first responders and other clinicians to further hone and perfect their craft.

THE HARTFORD CLUB

*In many ways, the history of **The Hartford Club** is the history of Hartford.*

Since 1873, some of New England's most influential people have lived, spent leisure time and held conversations that have shaped the city, state and region within its storied walls.

When the club was founded more than 135 years ago, it was not, by far, the first organization of its kind in the city. Among its founding members were William James Hamersley, whose firm Hamersley & Belknap published works by Horace Bushnell and Lydia Sigourney; his son William Hamersley, who founded the Connecticut Bar Association and served as state's attorney for more than 20 years before being appointed as a judge to the Supreme Court; and Charles M. Pond, who bequeathed Elizabeth Park — named for his wife — to the city of Hartford. By far, the club's most famous member was Samuel Clemens, who joined in 1881.

The Hartford Club is still committed to providing its members with a first-class venue to facilitate business and social needs. Member privileges include fine dining, elegant, residential-style banquet and meeting rooms, members' cigar and smoking lounge, a billiards room, special member activities and concierge-assisted services. The clubhouse is a private and elegant location for leaders in business, government, philanthropy and academia to comfortably gather and socialize. It is also an upscale venue for large parties, weddings, as well as small intimate dinners and gatherings. The private club experience is further enhanced by reciprocal privileges at more than 200 clubs worldwide. The club has also recently added the privileges of the ClubCorp network of private clubs, adding 200 more city, athletic and country clubs for members' use, as well as premier resorts such as Pinehurst and the Homestead.

Over the past few years the club has reached out to the community and provided associate memberships to the leaders of several area nonprofit organizations, allowing them to utilize the club facilities to host meetings and events. The membership is offered at no cost to the organizations, so it is not a draw on ever-tightening budgets. The club has also reached out to the young executive community in Hartford, whose members now constitute nearly one-fourth of the total membership. Partnering with the MetroHartford Alliance in a special membership program has also helped keep the club at the center of business activity in Hartford. The club's recent growth in membership across a broad spectrum is indicative of the future strength of The Hartford Club.

Above: An etching of the Hartford Club Entrance.

Right: a 'Tasteful Tasting.'

PHOTOGRAPHIC MOMENTS 153

Prudential Retirement

With more than 85 years of retirement experience, Prudential Retirement is one of the United States' leading providers.

Originally called the Prudential Friendly Society and later, the Prudential Insurance Company of America, Prudential Financial, Inc. was founded in 1875, in a basement office in downtown Newark, N.J., by John Fairfield Dryden.

The company began as an organization committed to making life insurance available and affordable to working-class Americans. From its humble beginnings, Prudential Financial, Inc. has grown into one of the most recognized brands in the world. Its well-known rock symbol is an icon of strength, stability, expertise and innovation in financial services that has stood the test of time.

Prudential Financial has more than 41,044 employees worldwide, while Prudential Retirement has 2,600 employees across the nation, with about 800 in Hartford as of December 31, 2010. Prudential Retirement's Chief Marketing Officer Kara Segreto says retirement security is what the group does best, and service remains the goal. "That's why we exist," she said. "That's why we're here. We're trying to focus more on what we deliver to institutions and individuals."

Prudential Financial, Inc. has been providing a variety of retirement plan products and services to institutions since the early 1920s. Prudential Retirement came to Hartford in 2004, after Prudential Financial's acquisition of CIGNA's retirement business.

With more than 85 years of retirement experience, Prudential Retirement is one of the United States' leading providers. As of June 30, 2011, its clients included 7,000 institutions that provide retirement plans to their employees and members, with nearly $221 billion in total account values. The company manages the retirement savings accounts of approximately 3.6 million individuals. Prudential Retirement's products and services are provided by Prudential Retirement Insurance and Annuity Company, Hartford, CT, or its affiliates.

Prudential Retirement prides itself on continually developing new products, tools and services to better meet the needs of plan sponsors and participants. Among these tools is the Retirement Income Calculator mobile app, which allows users to input information like their age, salary and current retirement savings and calculate an estimated monthly retirement income and estimated monthly retirement income need. The calculator — previously only available on the website — gives 2.6 million users instant access to their accounts. It's fun, engaging and instead of just a number or discouraging projections, the calculator offers hope in the form of an explanation and a personal action plan.

In November 2010, the company launched a new FDIC-insured product that is part of a 401(k) plan for employers and employees. Prudential Retirement is one of the first companies to offer such a product. Funds invested are considered deposits of Prudential Bank and Trust, FSB, member FDIC.

The company also offers an asset allocation program that assists plan participants in selecting investments that take into account their individual life stage, risk tolerance and retirement goals. In 2007, the company introduced a guaranteed income product. This innovative retirement-plan option can deliver lifetime retirement income while allowing participants to maintain total control of fund assets.

Along with day-to-day plan support, Prudential Retirement also keeps plan sponsors up-to-date on legislative issues and industry trends that may impact retirement savings through dedicated client relationship managers, consultants, and sponsor newsletters.

Unlike some other firms, Prudential Retirement met the financial crisis of 2008-2009 head-on, continuing to be a leader in the retirement services industry. "We retained our clients, we continued to innovate new products and solutions during a period of economic volatility," said Segreto. Prudential Retirement further showed its strength when it acquired the nation's leading nonqualified benefits provider, MullinTBG. Headquartered in California, it provides what are called non-qualified retirement plans for executives.

The company recently celebrated two major milestones. In June 2011, Prudential Retirement completed the first-ever pension-risk transfer sale to a U.S. plan sponsor and, one week later, completed its first longevity reinsurance transaction.

Yet Prudential Retirement is most proud of the incredible knowledge and talent of its employees. Their commitment to helping clients work toward a more secure future, as well as their volunteerism and support within the community are integral to its role as a strong civic advocate within and around Hartford. The company is proud of Hartford's growth and sense of community and its own association with the city and entire region.

The offices of Prudential Retirement are located at 280 Trumbull St., Hartford.

"Prudential Financial's long history of corporate citizenship is marked today by both our corporate philanthropy and the work our individual associates do to support their communities," said Christine Marcks, Prudential Retirement president. Prudential Retirement's employees spend thousands of hours each year donating their time and energy to dozens of community organizations in the Hartford area. The highlight of those activities is Prudential Financial's Global Volunteer Day, an annual event during which employees volunteer a day to help a wide variety of community organizations. The event occurs across Prudential Financial, and in 2010, more than 25,000 employees participated in more than 800 projects worldwide.

"This powerful combination of institutional and personal commitment is at the very heart of yet another important tenet of our organization: leadership," says Marcks. "And the community support provided by our associates is a shining example for all of us of the truest and best demonstration of leadership: service to others."

University of Hartford

The University of Hartford was founded by business and community leaders who envisioned a center of education and culture for central Connecticut.

Above: University of Hartford's Project Horizon health outreach project prepares professionals for service to the community.

Below: The Integrated Science, Engineering and Technology complex on the University of Hartford campus encourages cooperation across academic disciplines and promotes close student-faculty interaction.

From this vision evolved the private university's mission to have a public purpose, serving as a valued resource for individuals, businesses and communities, both locally and globally.

Today's University of Hartford is an economic engine in the Greater Hartford region. With nearly 1,100 employees, it is a $250 million-plus employer that attracts more than 4,600 undergraduate and 1,700 graduate students to campus each year.

BlumShapiro, the largest regional accounting, tax, and business consulting firm in New England, was lead funder of a first-ever study of the University's student spending habits. Conducted by a professor and students in the University's Barney School of Business in the spring of 2011, the study found that university students spend approximately $31.2 million annually in the three municipalities where the campus is located: Bloomfield, Hartford and West Hartford. This spending, in turn, stimulates $55.6 million in spending in the local economy. The study, which was also supported by the town of Bloomfield, eFollett.com college bookstores and Aramark food service, found that University of Hartford student spending supports nearly 500 jobs in the local economy.

The seven schools and colleges of the University of Hartford regularly seek and sustain partnerships with business and industry in the state. The College of Engineering, Technology, and Architecture (CETA) sees industry as an important partner in the university's ability to sustain excellence in engineering through education and applied research. CETA's Engineering Applications Center, which conducts applied research involving students, faculty and staff, is one of many collaborations between the University and major regional manufacturers.

The university's College of Education, Nursing and Health Professions has a long-standing commitment to preparing professionals for service to the community. Its partnerships with education, health, and community organizations include the Educational Main Street tutoring program and Project Horizon health services. Such external affiliations are vital to integrating health and education science with community engagement; they are exemplified by partnerships with the 36-school Hartford Public Schools system and the 617-bed Saint Francis Hospital and Medical Center in Hartford.

University of Hartford's Barney School of Business is committed to preparing leaders and decision makers who are globally aware and socially responsible. Whether leading major corporations, managing not-for-profit organizations, or starting businesses of their own, many Barney graduates are successfully contributing to the region's long-term economic health.

CAPEWELL COMPONENTS COMPANY LLC

Capewell Components Company LLC, originally founded as The Capewell Horse Nail Company by George J. Capewell, has been a part of the Connecticut manufacturing industry since 1881.

The company has been credited with the early invention of the automatic cold swaging process machine used to manufacture and shape nails.

Capewell Components's continued success over more than 130 years is attributed to its aspiration to provide new and innovative products to a global market to sustain an energy-efficient and safe society.

Today, with more than 150 dedicated employees, Capewell Components continues to grow and serve commercial, industrial and military markets in the US and worldwide. The company maintains its online presence at www.capewellcorp.com and is comprised of three divisions: Capewell, M.H. Rhodes Cramer and Ripley.

Capewell division, based in South Windsor, Conn., is a world leader in the design and manufacturer of life support and aerial delivery systems for the military and humanitarian relief efforts.

Capewell provides the total package of design, manufacturing, technical support and training to meet customers' demanding requirements. Capewell is ISO 9001 and AS9100 certified in conformance of Military specification and to ensure continuous improvement and provide the highest quality products to our customers.

M.H. Rhodes Cramer division, also based in South Windsor, Conn., has provided precision hand-crafted switches, timers and motors for commercial, industrial and residential markets since 1922.

MarkTime® brand timers and switches along with Cramer motorized cycle timers, fractional power motors, and hour meter product solutions are recognized worldwide and utilized in the aerospace, energy management, food service, HVAC, medical and warewasher industries.

Ripley division, based in Cromwell, Conn., is a recognized leader in design and manufacture of specialized and ergonomic wire and cable tools worldwide. For more than 30 years, professional lineman, technicians and installers have trusted Ripley tools, which are designed to promote safety and productivity in wire and cable preparation.

The European market is served by Ripley Europe, a U.K. subsidiary. Markets in the Far East are served by the Ripley office in China.

Ripley division, with its worldwide stocking distribution network, is the best single source for Cablematic®, Miller® and Utility Tool™ brand cable preparation tools.

"Capewell Components LLC is devoted to our Hartford heritage and our Connecticut employees," said company President Richard Wheeler. "We believe in the quality that our workers manufacture every day as we embrace new technologies, new markets, and a global economy."

Above: Views of the Capewell Components' South Windsor and Cromwell facilities.

Right: Products representing the three divisions of Capewell, from left to right: Capewell Components, M.H. Rhodes Cramer, and Ripley Co.

Northeast Utilities

Since Northeast Utilities and its companies were founded, we have built an enduring legacy of delivering reliable energy for our customers and leadership for our industry. We continue to build on that legacy with our support of the efficient use of energy and new clean energy technologies as a foundation for regional economic growth.

From the energy of our more than 6,000 employees, to the electric and natural gas energy we deliver to approximately 2 million customers in Connecticut, Western Massachusetts and New Hampshire, to anticipating the region's needs for renewable and low-carbon power, Northeast Utilities (NU) and its companies take our role supporting customers and communities with essential services very seriously. And we deliver on that commitment every day.

Our more than 100 years serving the Northeast have encompassed a sea of change. Today, customers use sophisticated computers and other electronic devices at home and work and businesses require unprecedented power quality and reliability. NU and its companies provide both the stability and flexibility to weather change and deliver innovative solutions to meet customers' changing energy needs. Our brand is built on that promise.

Since its founding, NU's primary role in delivering reliable energy service is unchanged. Our companies are also committed to contributing to economic growth in the communities they serve and to using their resources to be a leader in ways that are beneficial to the customer.

NU traces its roots back to the formation of its earliest predecessor companies in 1881 — only two years after Edison perfected the light bulb. The modern company was formally incorporated in 1966 through the merger of three companies: The Connecticut Light and Power Company (CL&P), the Hartford Electric Light Company (HELCO) and Western Massachusetts Electric Company (WMECo). In 1982, HELCO was merged into CL&P, a company serving about 1.2 million electric customers in 149 cities and towns in Connecticut.

NU's family of companies also include Public Service Company of New Hampshire, serving more than 490,000 electric customers in more than 200 communities; WMECo, meeting the daily energy needs of some 200,000 customers throughout 59 communities in Western Massachusetts; and Yankee Gas, serving approximately 200,000 customers in 71 Connecticut communities.

NU continues to grow and invest in its communities. Demonstrating its long-term commitment to Connecticut and its capital city, in 2009 NU moved its headquarters to downtown Hartford while retaining and fully utilizing its Berlin campus to serve the growing needs of CL&P, Yankee Gas and NU's transmission business.

In 2010, we capped the year with an agreement to merge with the Boston-area electric and gas utility NSTAR to ensure our position as New England's leading regional energy company. This transaction will provide a better platform for us to deliver on our promise for future growth.

The strategic and operational focus of NU and its companies is on investing to further upgrade, strengthen and modernize our energy distribution and transmission systems. For example, CL&P continues to develop a family of transmission projects to improve regional reliability

The headquarters of Northeast Utilities at 56 Prospect St., Hartford.

and provide a strong transmission connection for the flow of power throughout southern New England. Yankee Gas continues to expand Connecticut's energy options by increasing the availability of natural gas as a fuel of choice for its cleanliness, efficiency and reliability.

In addition, we continue to advance our growing portfolio of energy solutions to address New England's long-term energy and environmental goals. Recognizing future environmental challenges facing the region, NU has proposed new transmission solutions to increase access to renewable and low-carbon energy sources from northern New England and Canada, and to support the further development of wind power and biomass generation in our area.

However, NU is committed to more than just delivering energy for a changing world. Each NU company and its employees take an active role in the communities it serves: from volunteering at the individual level to being leaders in regional economic development.

During years of extended economic weakness and diminished resources for our cities and towns, NU has managed its costs and continues to be a stable employer of thousands of residents and a vital source of revenue for state and local governments. NU employs more than two-thirds of its workforce in Connecticut. Due to its expansive energy delivery system, NU is often the largest taxpayer in many of the communities it serves, providing $103.5 million in tax revenues to Connecticut in 2010 and $166 million across its three states.

Through its companies and employees, NU also provides critical financial support to nonprofit organizations struggling in the face of dwindling public and private resources. NU companies provided a total of $1.6 million to nonprofit and civic organizations in Connecticut in 2010 and a total of $2.5 million across its tri-state service territory.

As part of an innovative and significant commitment to the state, CL&P bought $7.4 million in tax credits in 2010 through the Connecticut Housing Finance Authority's Housing Tax Credit Contribution program to support housing programs across the state. The company followed that with over $15 million in State Historic Tax Credits purchased through Connecticut's Commission on Culture and Tourism.

The NU Foundation gave more than $2.2 million in 2010 to support initiatives in our customers' communities and donated $1 million last winter to support fuel assistance programs in Connecticut, Western Massachusetts and New Hampshire. CL&P and Yankee Gas are also ardent supporters of the Connecticut Energy Efficiency Fund, an initiative designed to make it easy for residents and businesses to use energy more efficiently in order to save money, energy and the environment.

The philanthropy of our companies is a reflection of our employees, who themselves pledged over $1.1 million to United Way chapters across our three states in 2010. NU employees also demonstrate their commitment to caring for their neighbors by taking part in the United Way's annual Day of Caring, often in record numbers.

At NU, we are doing more than imagining a better energy future — we are working to create one. Our scale and geographic reach give us a unique position to provide leadership that makes a difference in the region's energy landscape, both now and in the future.

Whether we are working to reduce our customers' carbon footprint or reaching out to policymakers, peer utilities and project developers about accessing new sources of renewable power, NU and its companies are prepared to face today's energy challenges and welcome the opportunities of tomorrow.

The familiar yellow trucks of Connecticut Light & Power, a Northeast Utilities company.

Charter Oak Insurance and Financial Services Co.

Charter Oak Insurance and Financial Services Co. — originally known as Massachusetts Mutual Life Insurance Company's (MassMutual) Springfield agency — has been servicing the risk management, insurance, business planning and protection, retirement planning and investment services needs of individuals, families and businesses for 125 years.

Clockwise from top: Brendan Naughton, General Agent; Peter Novak, General Agent; Joanna Leary, Marketing and Communications Director; Brett Amendola, Managing Director; Michelle Ransom, Agency Investment Specialist gather for a morning meeting.

We are one of the largest general agencies of MassMutual, which opened its doors in 1851. Today MassMutual is ranked as one of the most admired companies in the life and health industry by Fortune Magazine (March 21, 2011). Our relationship with MassMutual makes us proud to be part of a long history of exceptional strength, growth, quality and integrity. MassMutual is a mutually owned company, operating for the benefit of its members and participating policyholders. Throughout the most prosperous and turbulent of financial times, its mutual ownership structure has been the foundation of its business strategy. MassMutual is managed with the long-term interests of its policyholders and customers in mind, helping to ensure right decisions are made today so we are to meet the needs of policyholders in the future.

Since our own beginnings in 1886, we've expanded to offices in Farmington, Hamden, Southbury and Stamford, Conn., as well as in Holyoke, Mass. The span of our locations puts us close to financial and business centers in both New York and Boston and allows us to serve a variety of clientele, from sports and entertainment figures and large institutional companies to small businesses and the everyday consumer. Our unique combination of local presence and regional resources means our clients and business associates receive one-on-one service, backed by the power of many.

The agency's longevity has been marked by success. Charter Oak is a perennial winner of MassMutual's prestigious Chairman's Trophy Award, and its agents and leadership are regularly recognized both within MassMutual and by leading industry organizations. With more than $3.6 billion in client policy and account values(1) and nearly $12 billion in life insurance coverage in force(2), we continue to grow in ways that help us better serve our clients and communities.

Our People Make the Difference

We recognize that our ability to help those around us wouldn't be possible without our dedicated team of agents and employees. Our more than 200 professionals are parents, former athletes and coaches, business owners, CEOs, journalists, musicians, members of the military and scholars, to name a few. We believe the diversity of our experiences helps us to better understand the unique situations our clients face every day. It also creates a rich and engaging workplace for our employees. In fact, our workplace culture has earned us a spot among the Best Places to Work in Connecticut by the *Hartford Business Journal* and the Best Companies Group, an honor we will strive to repeat year after year.

Charter Oak's leadership continues to be a steady and driving force behind the agency's growth and accomplishments. Since appointing our first general agent on June 1, 1886, we have had only six changes in leadership, including the appointments of current general agents Peter Novak and Brendan Naughton. We believe this stability has allowed us to land on our feet during some of history's most difficult and uncer-

From L-R: Charter Oak General Agents Brendan Naughton and Pete Novak are among only six changes in leadership the agency has undergone in the past 125 years.

Fall oaks in a local park. Charter Oak took its name for the legend of the Charter Oak, which purports that our Colonial forebears hid Connecticut's constitutional charter in the cavity of an oak tree to thwart royal-ordered confiscation by English authority.

tain times — and helped us rise to the top in periods of prosperity.

Doing Well By Doing Good

We are proud to reinforce our commitment to the people we serve through the Charter Oak Fund, our philanthropic arm. Our most recent contributions have gone to organizations within Central and Southern Connecticut and Western Massachusetts that offer services for children with special needs. Our multiyear financial and volunteer support has helped bolster crucial programming for these children, and has given us the opportunity to form lasting, meaningful relationships with their families and services providers.

Stronger Together

We believe that our relationship with our clients, our associates and the communities around us is about much more than financial services and insurance. It's about children and parents, brothers and sisters, businesses and employees. It's listening to what others have to say and putting their interests first. It's being a part of a team and a member of the community.

Back when business was still done on a handshake and a sense of trust and partnership prevailed, collaborations like this were common. A lot has changed since those days, but we still believe what was true then is true now: we are stronger together than we are alone.

We remain connected to this philosophy in all that we do.

Securities, investment advisory and financial planning services offered through qualified registered representatives of MML Investors Services LLC, Member SIPC. Supervisory office: 76 Batterson Park Road, Farmington, CT 06032. 860-674-1800.

(1) All information as of 03/01/11. Includes values of MassMutual and subsidiary insurance companies' insurance and retirement products and investment products offered through MML Investors Services LLC, a MassMutual subsidiary.

(2) Amount of individual life insurance in force at the end of the period related to products issued by Massachusetts Mutual Life Insurance Co. and its subsidiaries, C.M. Life Insurance Co. and MML Bay State Life Insurance Co. CRN201309-152235

Saint Francis Hospital and Medical Center

Saint Francis Hospital and Medical Center is a major teaching hospital with 617 licensed inpatient beds, 65 bassinets and five centers of excellence that embrace patients at every stage of a lifetime.

Saint Francis Hospital and Medical Center has come a long way in the 114 years since the Sisters of Saint Joseph of Chambéry overcame near-impossible odds to open a two-room hospital in Hartford's Asylum Hill neighborhood. The new hospital offered a refuge for immigrants who wanted to know that their faith and traditions would be understood and appreciated if they ever needed inpatient care.

From the beginning, Saint Francis served on the front lines against outbreaks of then-deadly infectious diseases, from typhoid fever to influenza and later polio. At the same time, Saint Francis doctors were quick to recognize that improving health required more than clinical work. The first research laboratory opened in 1902, the same year that tuberculosis was reaching epic proportions in Hartford and across the United States.

Typhoid to High-Tech

While better sanitation, vaccines and antibiotics have tamed many of the early killers, Saint Francis is even busier today, tackling the healthcare threats and ailments of the modern world with technology and medical interventions that the founding sisters could not even imagine. But the very tenets upon which the hospital was founded — clinical excellence coupled with compassionate caring — have never changed.

In 1990, Saint Francis affiliated with Mount Sinai Hospital, a Jewish-sponsored institution that opened in 1923. Mount Sinai was born of a vision similar to the one that led to the founding of Saint Francis decades earlier. This new collaboration marked the first recorded instance of a Catholic and Jewish hospital affiliation in United States history. The arrangement was formalized as a corporate merger in 1995.

As the needs of Connecticut residents evolve, so does Saint Francis. In 2011, the John T. O'Connell Tower opened its doors. Ten stories high, the tower features a new emergency department with 70 treatment areas, 13 sheltered ambulance bays, and a rooftop helipad. The upper floors are home to 19 new operating rooms and 135 private patient rooms, including two floors dedicated to orthopedics.

From a fledgling hospital with 32 patients in a ward, Saint Francis has grown into New England's largest Catholic hospital, with 617 licensed inpatient beds, 65 bassinets and five centers of excellence that embrace patients at every stage of life.

Centers of Excellence

A regional referral center and major teaching hospital, Saint Francis provides sophisticated, contemporary medicine with major clinical concentrations in women's and children's services, oncology, cardiology, orthopedics, and rehabilitation.

In Expert Hands

Women and Children: Caring for women and children begins before conception and extends beyond retirement. Labor and delivery, gynecological care and comprehensive breast health are flagship programs of the *Women's and Children's Health* program. The *New Beginnings Family Birth Care* model provides a unique birthing experience for each mother and her family. It offers enhanced privacy features, attractive and comfortable surroundings, and the latest medical technology. Facilities include:

- Fourteen labor/delivery/recovery rooms
- Thirty private post-partum suites
- A 26-bassinet well-baby nursery
- A 28-bassinet Level III neonatal intensive care unit (NICU)
- Two Cesarean-section delivery rooms
- A state-of-the-art antepartum diagnostic center

Below: Aerial view of Saint Francis Hospital and Medical Center's main campus.

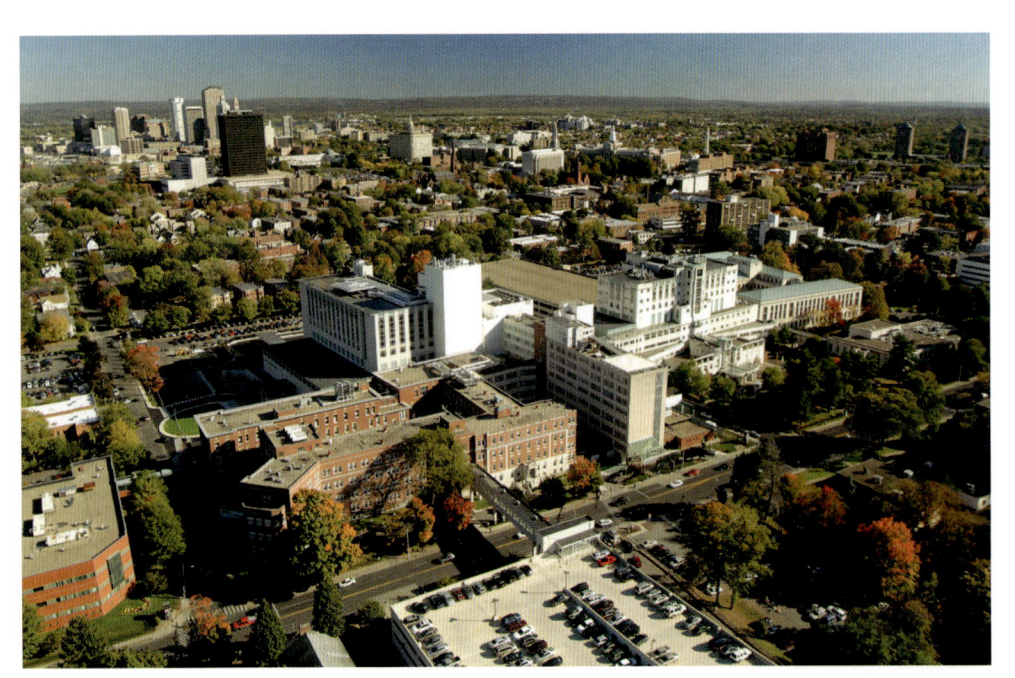

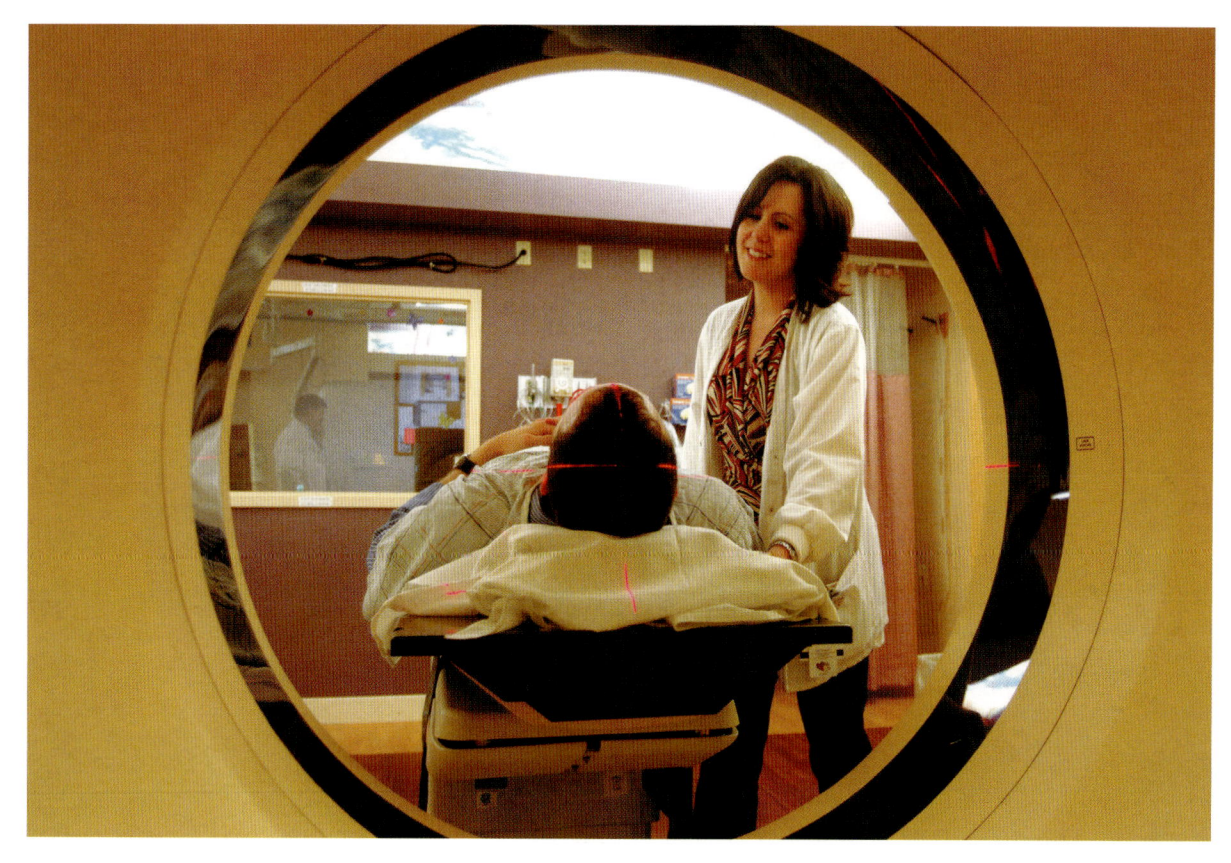

Left: A patient at Saint Francis/Mount Sinai Regional Cancer Center undergoes a CT scan in preparation for radiation therapy.

Below: A nurse tends to a preemie in the NICU at Saint Francis Hospital and Medical Center. The New Beginnings Family Birth Care Center is a cornerstone of Women's and Children's services, which also include expert breast and gynecological care for women at every stage of life.

Delivery by a nurse midwife is among the options available. Saint Francis midwives approach pregnancy as a healthy, empowering experience. Each prenatal visit is tailored to meet the physical, emotional, and informational needs of the woman and her family.

When gynecological problems arise, expert surgeons and minimally invasive technologies, including daVinci® robotic surgery, offer quicker recovery with better outcomes. At the *Comprehensive Breast Health Center*, women with routine, as well as complex breast health concerns benefit from our streamlined approach to breast cancer prevention, diagnosis, treatment and recovery. The discomfort of a mammogram aside, many women agree that waiting for the results is the hardest part. That's why the breast center at Saint Francis never makes women wait. As soon as an exam is complete, the digital x-ray is transmitted to an on-site radiologist who reads it and reports the results immediately. Every woman who has a mammogram at Saint Francis leaves the center knowing whether she can breathe easy for another year or if she needs more follow-up.

High-tech, Comforting Touch

Saint Francis/Mount Sinai Regional Cancer Center is one of New England's leading outpatient cancer treatment centers, providing the latest technology and the most comprehensive range of treatment options in the region. More than 1,500 cancer patients and their families depend on the *Saint Francis/Mount Sinai Regional Cancer Center* every year. A team approach distinguishes the *Saint Francis/Mount Sinai Regional Cancer Center*. Specialists — medical, surgical, radition, rehabilitation and others — can see each patient in a single visit. This innovative, one-stop approach streamlines the diagnosis and consultation process, allowing patients to move forward with a timely and comprehensive treatment plan. Individualized care plans can include a combination of conventional and investigational therapies through our access to more than 100 National Cancer Institute-funded clinical trials. In addition, state-of-the-art radiation therapy techniques offer patients a wide variety of non-surgical options for cancer treatment. With CyberKnife® and the most up-to-date linear accelerators, *Saint Francis/Mount Sinai Regional Cancer Center* is equipped with gold-standard technology to treat a wide variety of cancers.

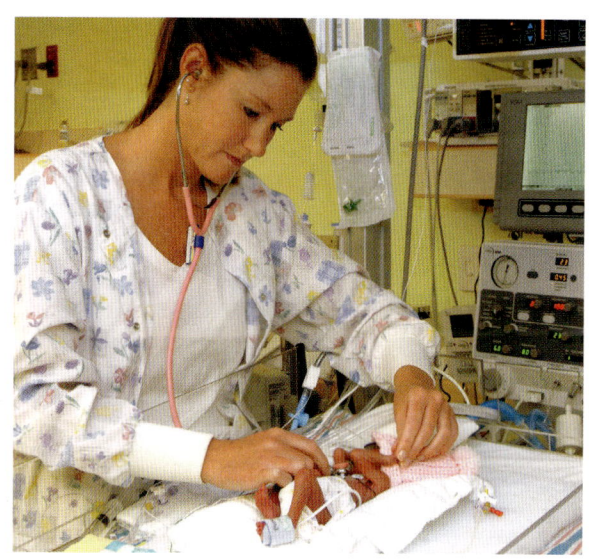

Continued on next page

SAINT FRANCIS HOSPITAL AND MEDICAL CENTER

Continued from previous page

Leading-edge, Leading the Way

The Hoffman Heart and Vascular Institute of Connecticut is the largest open-heart surgery center in the state. In emergencies, Saint Francis delivers the fastest response to heart attack in the area. The institute also is among the highest-volume cardiac catheterization programs in the region—a fact that directly correlates with saving lives. With state-of-the-art technology, Saint Francis cardiologists can also correct heart rhythm disorders and manage patients with advanced congestive heart failure. The institute's electrophysiology laboratories are equipped with Stereotaxis® magnet-guided catheter technology, which allows treatment of atrial fibrillation and other arrhythmias with pinpoint accuracy and increased safety. Because heart disease is the leading cause of death in women, the *Phillips Women's Heart Program at Saint Francis* is a risk-reduction and education program for women designed to prevent heart attack and stroke. It is free to women over the age of 18, and includes an individualized risk assessment and a two-hour education session provided by a registered nurse, a registered dietician and an exercise physiologist.

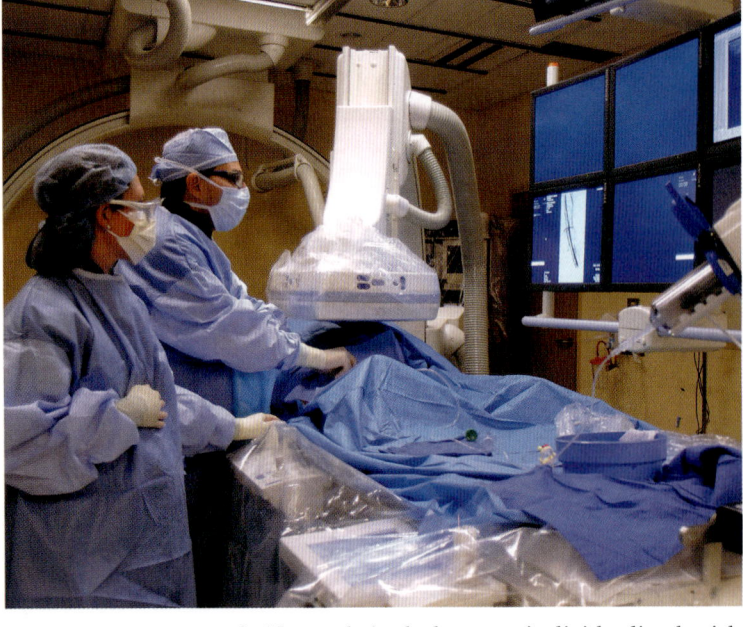

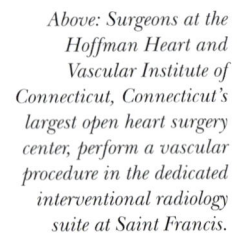

Experience: The Difference

The Connecticut Joint Replacement Institute (CJRI) is the newest of Saint Francis' centers of excellence, having opened its doors in 2007. Led by fellowship-trained orthopedic surgeons and located in the new John T. O'Connell Tower, *CJRI* is a "hospital within a hospital," with dedicated operating rooms and staff for hip- and knee-replacement surgeries. *CJRI* is recognized as one of the major arthritis and joint replacement centers on the East Coast, offering:

- Board-certified, orthopedic-trained surgeons
- Multidisciplinary teams working together to provide expert care for patients needing joint replacement procedures
- A pre-assessment surgical screening center to ensure that medical issues have been identified and addressed prior to surgery
- Multidisciplinary patient education pre-operative classes, held weekly

In addition to direct patient care, the staff of *CJRI* is involved in research in materials used in joint replacement surgery and in post-operative pain control. Given the aging baby boomer generation, the need for joint replacement procedures is expected to grow substantially nationwide by 2030. *CJRI* is well positioned to meet that need. CJRI is the largest joint replacement center in Connecticut.

Above: Surgeons at the Hoffman Heart and Vascular Institute of Connecticut, Connecticut's largest open heart surgery center, perform a vascular procedure in the dedicated interventional radiology suite at Saint Francis.

Right: Physical therapy, one of many services available at the Mount Sinai Rehabilitation Hospital, helps patients regain movement and function following a serious illness or injury.

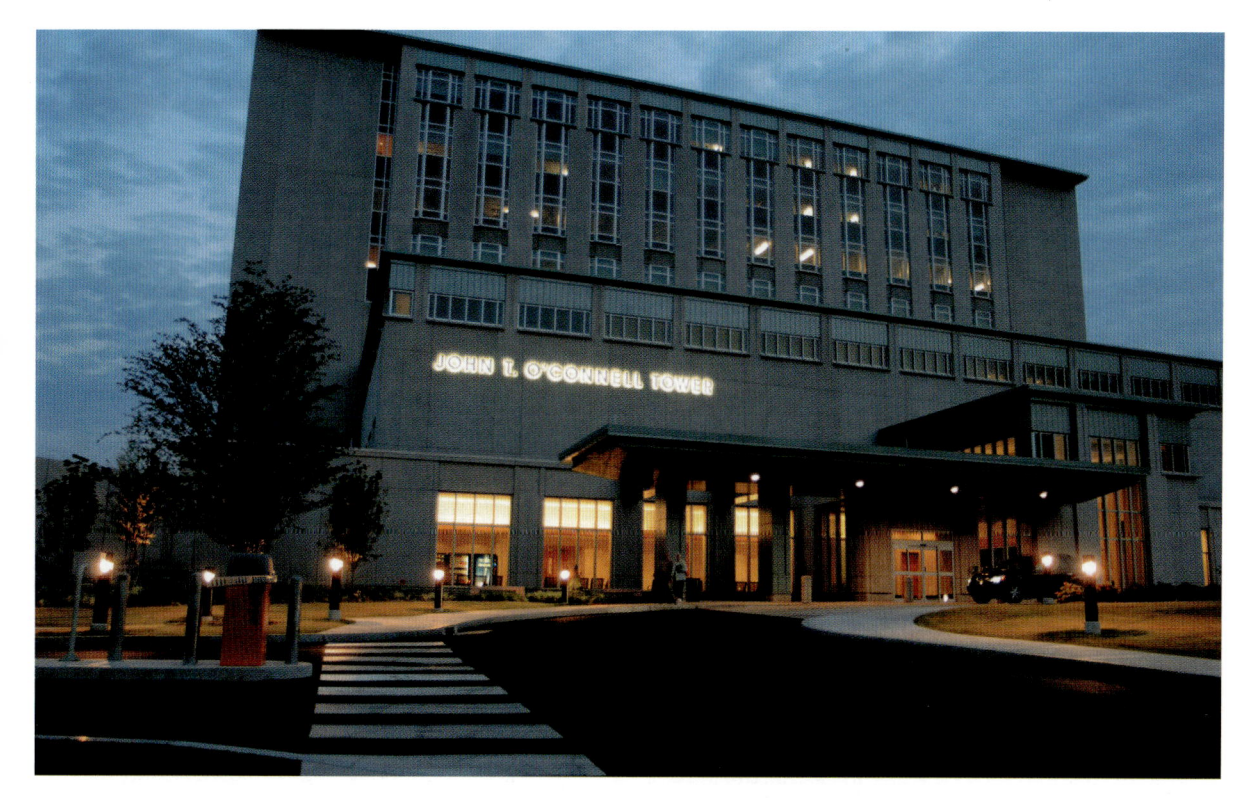

Left: In 2011, Saint Francis Hospital and Medical Center expanded its Hartford campus with the John T. O'Connell Tower, a 10-story building that is home to a new emergency department, 19 new operating rooms and 135 private patient rooms.

A Tradition of Innovation

Mount Sinai Rehabilitation Hospital is located on the campus of the former Mount Sinai Hospital in Hartford's North End. The 60-bed facility is Connecticut's only freestanding acute care rehabilitation hospital. Its focus is to restore the lives of people following serious illness or injury through programs for traumatic brain injury, stroke/neurological rehabilitation, sports medicine, spinal cord injuries and orthopedics. In addition, it offers rehabilitation services for patients who have become debilitated following a serious illness or a long hospital stay. The rehabilitation team also works closely with the staff of the *Joyce D. and Andrew J. Mandell Center for Comprehensive Multiple Sclerosis Care and Neuroscience Research*. The center provides MS patients with services that were not previously available in the region, including a unique robotic walking system known as the Lokomat®, now being applied in specialized MS research.

Full-Service, First-Rate

In addition to its centers of excellence, Saint Francis offers a full range of expert medical and dental care with respected programs in:

- Stroke care
- General Surgery
- Surgical weight loss
- Diabetes management
- Orthopedic and sports medicine
- Pain management
- Integrative medicine

Moving Forward

In the same way that Saint Francis honors the legacy of the Sisters of Saint Joseph through its mission of compassionate care, the hospital is always looking ahead to anticipate better ways to deliver that care in a rapidly changing healthcare environment. Responding to the dynamics of the changing marketplace, the hospital recently adopted a five-year strategic plan designed to position it for future growth. The plan sets forth a road map for delivering on its promise of Best*Care* for a Lifetime℠.

Toward that end, a patient-centered model of care has been envisioned to produce the perfect patient experience and the highest measurable quality across the continuum of care needed by our community.

From its humble beginnings, Saint Francis has continuously responded to the community's evolving healthcare needs through a combination of the best clinical care, the best training of health care professionals, top-level research and community support. Together, these principles have allowed Saint Francis to build a 114-year tradition of providing the Best*Care* for a Lifetime.

Visit Saint Francis Hospital and Medical Center on the web at www.stfranciscare.com. To find a Saint Francis physician, call 1-877-STFRANCIS (1-877-783-7262)

Leonard Hellerman

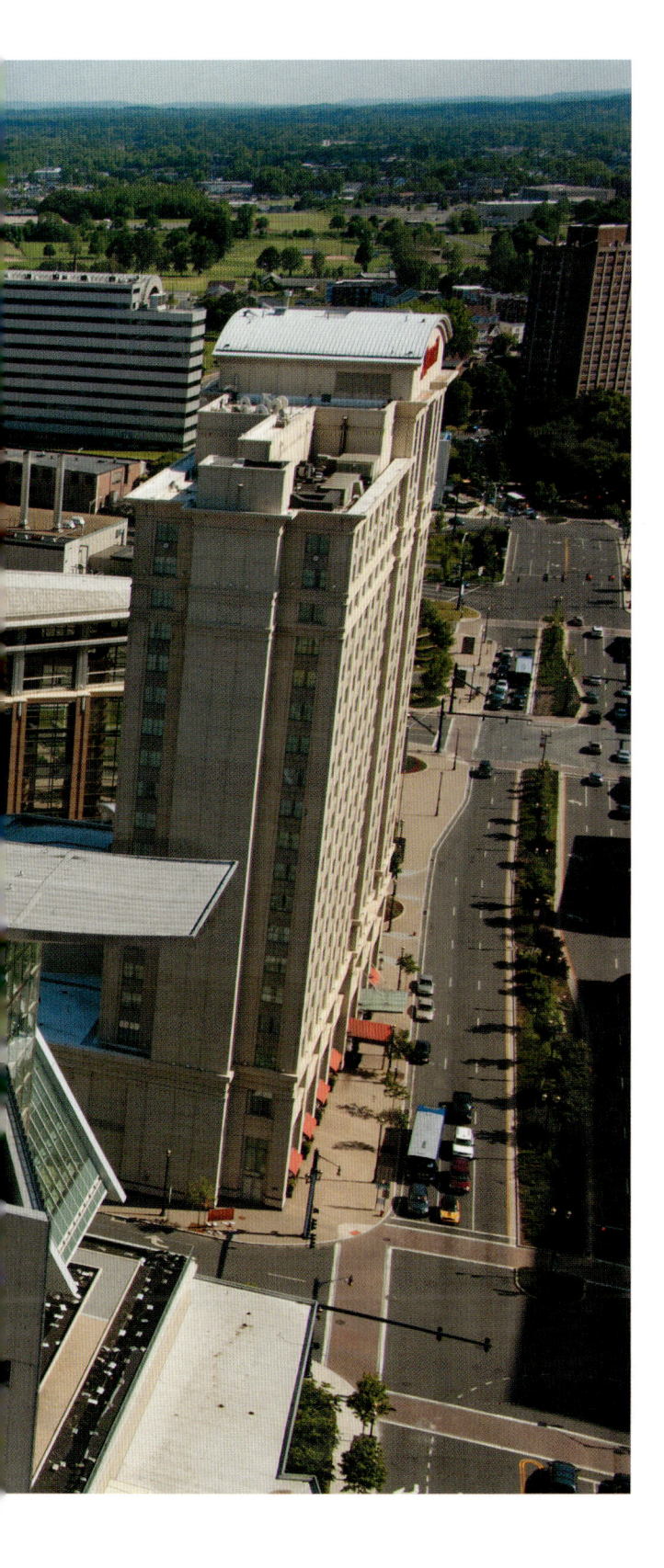

Profiles In Excellence
1910-2006

Year Founded	Company Name	Page Number
1910	Channel 3 Kids Camp	168
1925	The Town and County Club	169
1932	Saint Joseph College	170
1936	Nutmeg State Federal Credit Union	172
1942	The Associated Construction Company	174
1959	The Simon Konover Company	176
1968	Suburban Companies	177
1969	TRUMPF Inc.	178
1974	UnitedHealth Group	180
1978	Horton International LLC	182
1981	Stockton Associates	183
1981	LAZ Parking	184
1989	The Governor's Prevention Partnership	186
1992	Carousel Industries	188
1992	Charles Wareham and Associates/LPL Financial	190
1992	Hartford Business Journal	191
1995	Oakleaf Waste Management	192
1999	Cox Business	195
1999	Goodwin College	196
2003	Rider Productions LLC	198
2006	Camilliere, Cloud & Kennedy	200

Channel 3 Kids Camp

Camp programs aren't only about recreation. More than anything, Channel 3 Kids Camp teaches our children about life and how to live it well.

Camp is an experience every child deserves, regardless of their ability to pay. Realizing that there were hundreds of children in the Hartford area that would never be able to experience a country vacation and all the benefits to their health and well-being, the Harrison B. Freeman family, in collaboration with the Union for Home Work in Hartford, began its tradition of providing summer camping experiences for city children at their Andover, Connecticut, summer home — the Almada Lodge — in 1910.

In 1920, The Hartford Times newspaper assumed full responsibility for the program. In 1931, the Freeman family deeded the property, and the Hartford Times deeded the buildings, equipment and land, to a newly formed 501(c)(3) charitable corporation: The Almada Lodge–Times Farm Camp Corporation. Since 1976, WFSB Channel TV-3 has assisted the camp by raising awareness as a media sponsor and advertising for fundraising events.

Through the remarkable generosity of the public and other funding sources, the camp has grown from serving 20 campers in 1910 to serving more than 4,500 annually. Each year children ages 6-16 from every county in Connecticut and areas throughout New England attend the Channel 3 Kids Camp. The unique program welcomes boys and girls from all walks of life, but primarily those who typically do not have the financial ability to experience the joys and value of a high-quality program.

Camp opportunities are unmatched anywhere in the state, with year-round programs including: Summer Day & Overnight Camp; Teen Leadership Program; Camp Ventures After School Program; Nature's Classroom, a residential environmental education program for area schools; Winter Vacation Camp; Foster Reconnection Camp for separated siblings; National Military Family Association's Operation Purple, welcoming children of parents in the military; Camp Abilities CT, a developmental sports camp for children who are visually impaired, blind, or deaf-blind; and weekend retreats.

Over the past 101 years, the Channel 3 Kids Camp has improved the lives of more than 100,000 children through multiple, year-round programs on its 350 acres along the Skungamaug River. As the camp moves into its second century of service, its master plan outlines a Camp for All Children. The Kids Camp will continue to be a sanctuary for children regardless of economic, physical or developmental ability to come play, learn and grow without barriers.

"With the support of The Ashway Foundation, we have plans to build and open a new building named Ashley's Place," said Executive Director Denise Hornbecker. "More than 1,000 additional children will join us as we open the Camp for All Children at Ashley's Place during its first year of operation in 2013."

As it expands and transforms programs to meet the changing needs of campers, some things will never change; the Channel 3 Kids Camp will always be the one place in Connecticut everyone can count on to provide great experiences for our children. For more information visit www.channel3kidscamp.org or call (860) 742-2267.

Above: Channel 3 Kids Camp ropes course is an opportunity for campers to develop self-esteem, trust in their own ability and experience team building in a non-threatening environment. The course is just one of the many activities that are part of a comprehensive program stressing health, safety, well-being and cooperation.

Right: More than 100 years old, the Almada Lodge Times Farm Camp has consistently and successfully offered an accessible and inclusive camping experience for all children and youth throughout the region and from a variety of backgrounds.

The Town and County Club

The Town and County Club is here for today's women and the Hartford community.

In 1925 a group of 400 progressive and determined women committed their resources to form Hartford's first private women's city club. They purchased the grand 1895 Theodore Lyman house at 22 Woodland Street and created an organized center for social, intellectual and artistic gatherings.

In the 87 years since then, members of the Town and County Club have made significant contributions to the Greater Hartford community and beyond through their personal and professional connections. Their common interests are reinforced by the warm and welcoming atmosphere of their club house, where friendship, gourmet food and stimulating programs abound in a gracious setting.

If you ask members why they value the Town and County Club, you will hear many reasons. It is a place we forge and rekindle friendships; a home away from home; we have access to reciprocal clubs in the U.S. and abroad; and there is a full calendar of interesting programs and activities.

In 2010-2011, for example, dinner speakers included Dr. Robert Ballard, the renowned explorer of deep oceans; Prof. Donald Fisher, an authority on earthquakes and tsunamis; and Dr. Christina Kishimoto, Hartford's superintendent of public schools. Members and guests listened to jazz and chamber music and hosted new Hartford Symphony Orchestra conductor Carolyn Kuan. We discussed books and current events, formed a writing-for-pleasure group and played bridge. Our committees arranged monthly art exhibits and planned day trips.

Gracious hospitality and fine dining are hallmarks of the club. The Lyman House — with its rich 19th-century architectural details and the updated elegance of its furnishings — provides an upscale venue as a dining destination for members, their families, friends and colleagues. The ballroom — which has a superb floor for dancing — was added to the original house in 1930 and offers space for weddings, private social gatherings and business and charitable meetings and events.

From the beginning, members have reached out to the community.

In 1999 the club established a donor-advised fund at the Hartford Foundation for Public Giving and began awarding scholarships to adult women enrolled at Hartford-area colleges. Since then, dozens of scholarships have been awarded, creating a legacy of giving and an example of women helping women achieve their dreams.

In 2007, nonprofit 501(c)(3) status was granted to the Lyman Heritage Preservation Foundation. Tax-deductible gifts ensure preservation and enhancement of the historic house and grounds.

Today the Town and County's vital and diverse membership of more than 400 women and men perpetuates the mission of its founders to "create and maintain an environment for its members which fosters cultural, intellectual and social development."

Thanks to the vision of its members, the house and club thrive today. Visit www.towncounty.com and see for yourself.

Above: The Lyman House at the Town & County Club.

Below: The Library at the Town & County Club.

Saint Joseph College

Saint Joseph College blends academic excellence with a values-based approach to education that fosters diverse, innovative learning opportunities which extend into the broader community.

Saint Joseph College is a comprehensive institution offering more than 22 majors and six pre-professional programs plus accelerated bachelor's to master's degrees. Responsive to the evolving educational needs of the community, the College offers men and women graduate degree programs both online and in the classroom. In addition, SJC's Weekend Program for Adult Learners provides an undergraduate degree program, while professional certificate programs relevant to today's workforce are also available. In August 2011, the Saint Joseph College School of Pharmacy, the College's first doctoral program, welcomed its inaugural class to Hartford 21 on Trumbull Street in downtown Hartford. Pictured here: McDonough Hall on the campus of Saint Joseph College in West Hartford.

"This is a 21st century institution: growing, thriving, and forward-thinking," says Dr. Pamela Trotman Reid, president of Saint Joseph College (SJC). Founded in 1932 by the Sisters of Mercy as a college for women, today more than half of SJC's 2,500 students are enrolled in co-educational doctorate, master's, certificate and adult education programs, some of which are offered online. The traditional undergraduate program is the only four-year women's program in Connecticut, offering a unique experience for 850 full-time and 200 part-time students.

"Saint Joseph College is one of a kind," says Na-Tasha Bryan, Class of 2013. "I really love the small community we have here. All of the professors are willing to go out of their way to help you." Na-Tasha is majoring in social work with a minor in political science. She plans to get her MSW and then go on to law school. "A lot more can be done to make the world a better place," she commented in a video featured on the college's YouTube channel. Na-Tasha feels that her experience at SJC has given her the tools not only to take charge of her own destiny, but to help others as well.

The top reason students choose SJC (according to a survey conducted by the College in 2008) is for the quality of its academic programs. *U.S. News & World Report* ranked the College in the top tier of regional colleges in the northeast in 2011. Another important factor for students is the opportunity to grow in a supportive environment. "They feel a sense of community, that this is a warm and nurturing place where they can be successful, take risks, and learn things beyond what they ever thought they could do," observed Reid. "Students may be unassuming at first," added Cynthia Mariani, director of marketing and communications, "but by the time they leave they have found their voice and are ready to take on the world."

SJC's academic programs are offered through the schools of Education; Graduate and Professional Studies; Health and Natural Sciences; Humanities and Social Sciences; and Pharmacy. Many programs offer students opportunities for real-world experience in the community. Additionally, the College has two laboratory schools that give students in a number of disciplines first-hand observational and practicum experiences. The Gengras Center, a school for children with special needs, serves 125 students from 52 communities in Connecticut. The School for Young Children, a nationally-accredited preschool program, was one of the first preschools in the state and one of the first student laboratory programs in the nation.

In the fall of 2011, Saint Joseph College launched its first doctoral program, welcoming an inaugural class of

67 students to the Pharm.D. program at the School of Pharmacy. "There's a great national need due to a shortage of pharmacists. This program builds on our strengths in the sciences, and on our outstanding reputation within the health care community from our nursing and nutrition programs," says President Reid. According to *Forbes Magazine*, pharmacy is one of the highest paying careers for women, and the field is growing at a rate of 17 percent per year. The School of Pharmacy expects to enroll up to 100 students each year.

Housed in a state-of-the-art facility in downtown Hartford, the program is the only private school of pharmacy in the state. Featuring the Kathleen B. and Gene F. Bruyette Classroom in the Round (a high-tech classroom), the facility supports an intensive learning environment for students and close interaction with faculty. The School of Pharmacy has adopted a non-traditional modular schedule that is spread over three full years, rather than the typical four-year program. Students cover topics by organ systems, one at a time. "A professor teaches about the respiratory system, for example, in an integrated way, covering the anatomy, diseases, drug treatments and associated adverse effects, and patient counseling," explains Reid. Students spend time in clinical settings throughout the three years, applying what they learn in pharmacies and health care facilities.

Another logical extension of Saint Joseph's core strengths in health sciences is the College's professional doctorate program in nurse practice (DNP), which is currently being finalized. "Our largest undergraduate program is nursing, and we also offer the master's level," says Reid. "Today, individuals with a nurse practitioner degree can work independently and write prescriptions. But as the world and the health care system have gotten more complex, nurses need more education to provide advanced level patient care."

Central to the mission of SJC and all of its academic programs is a long-standing commitment to helping others. SJC was named to the Presidential Honor Roll for Community Service in 2009, 2010 and 2011. The College promotes a culture of service, with students participating in volunteer activities to support the needs of a variety of causes. Every College-sponsored club and organization is required to complete a service project. Students regularly organize fundraisers and donation drives. Each March a contingent of students use their spring break to participate in charitable projects in different areas of the country. The College's Guyana Immersion Experience works with the Guyanese Sisters of Mercy to give students in a number of majors the opportunity participate in academic and service activities with Guyanese students, while also conducting research. Mercy Week is an annual tradition in which members of the College community engage in service activities throughout the Greater Hartford region.

The original vision of the Sisters of Mercy lives on at the SJC campus. As the College builds on its success and expands into new areas, its focus on academic excellence blended with a values-based approach to education has not diminished, and its legacy of deep and enduring positive impact continues to grow. These values thrive in the beauty of its tree-lined campus and within the warmth of its nurturing and secure community. Additionally, Saint Joseph College has built upon its commitment to diversity, and is now one of the most diverse comprehensive institutions in Connecticut.

Above: Students seeking careers in health care or the biomedical sciences benefit greatly from the rigorous academic programs and faculty expertise.

Below: The Saint Joseph College School of Pharmacy, located at Hartford 21 on Trumbull Street in downtown Hartford, includes the Kathleen B. and Gene F. Bruyette Classroom in the Round, a technology-focused, interdisciplinary center of education, knowledge sharing and special events created by a $1 million gift from the Bruyettes, longtime benefactors of Saint Joseph College.

Nutmeg State Federal Credit Union

Community-based credit unions like Nutmeg State Federal Credit Union are becoming a popular choice for people who are tired of being treated more like a number than a person by large, inflexible, impersonal banks.

Credit unions offer the same range of financial products and services as banks, but are structurally and philosophically different. Credit unions are not-for-profit and owned by the people who bank there. "Credit unions do things to create value for their account holders, while banks do things to create value for their share holders," said John Holt, president and CEO of Nutmeg State Federal Credit Union. "The money that we make goes back into the credit union for things like new technology, new branches, higher rates on deposit accounts, and lower rates on loans," said Holt. "Everything we do is for the individuals and the communities we serve."

Nutmeg was founded in 1936 as Hartford Telephone Federal Credit Union and served employees and retirees of the Southern New England Telephone Company, which is now AT&T. In 2006, the organization expanded its charter to a community-based model and opened their doors to a broader segment of the population, making it possible for just about anyone to take advantage of the credit union's excellent products, rates and service.

Holt's vision for Nutmeg is to make it one of the premier financial institutions in Connecticut. "My plan is to double the size of the credit union in the next three to five years," he said. The pillars of his growth strategy are service and convenience. "We want our culture to be about building relationships and making it convenient for everyone to bank here," said Holt. Nutmeg, under Holt's leadership, expects to attract new business by offering a superior level of service and personal attention that is typically not found in larger banks. "When you walk through the doors of any of our branches, we want you to feel at home," said Holt. "Our focus on service, plus a culture of fitting each individual with the product that meets his or her specific needs, makes us unique."

Nutmeg has branches in Rocky Hill, Manchester, New Britain, East Windsor, Hartford, Glastonbury and Newington and plans to expand their branch network even further within the next 5 years to include locations in both Middlesex and Tolland counties. The credit union's Newington branch is located in a Price Chopper, a move unique among most other credit union branch strategies because it is the first credit union in the state to have a location in a grocery store. All locations offer the convenience of evening and weekend hours, as well as easy accessibility on all levels, whether in a branch or online.

Convenience across all channels is a major thrust of the organization, which is why Nutmeg offers services such as online banking, text message and e-mail alerts, and mobile banking apps on popular devices including iPhone, BlackBerry and Android. Their goal is to make it possible for people to have 24/7 access to their accounts whether it's during regular business hours or after hours online. Anyone can also open accounts and apply for loans online, and deposit checks from remote locations anytime day or night without having to ever physically deliver the check to the credit union.

Nutmeg is also dedicated to contributing and having a positive impact within the community. "We believe that by reinvesting in the community, we create and foster a better place to work and live," said Holt. As a credit union, Nutmeg encourages employees to get involved on a local and regional level. They've even introduced business savings, checking and loans in order to

Welcome sign in Rocky Hill

become a reliable resource for small, local businesses within the community.

"We want to be the most trusted local financial institution of choice," said Holt. "This is why our tagline is The One for Everyone. We actively reach out to all segments of the population, offering products and services that match their needs." To attract Gen-Y, Nutmeg offers a checking account for 13-17 year olds. This account provides the convenience of an ATM/Debit card and other electronic services, while also offering the security and peace of mind that parents seek. Additionally, the credit union offers a first-time car buyer loan and a credit builder loan to help younger people begin building good credit, and has developed an educational outreach program within local schools. For the Hispanic community, they have a Spanish-language version of their website, and marketing materials available. The organization is also actively reaching out to the gay and lesbian community. "We mean the fact that we want to be there to make everyone feel comfortable when they walk in the door, and that's what it's ultimately all about," said Holt. One of the principles of credit unions is to serve a diverse demographic, and Nutmeg exemplifies this philosophy. "We want to reach out to the markets that a lot of people don't pay attention to," Holt said. "We want to work with everyone."

A credit union's purpose is to provide financial products and services to those who need them, at fair and competitive rates and prices. Nutmeg still adheres to this principle. In a time of economic turmoil brought on by careless money management and focus on profits — not people — this old-fashioned philosophy, coupled with Nutmeg's strong commitment to the local community, makes this credit union an oasis of principled financial management that everyone can put their trust in and rely on for life. They are The One for Everyone.

Above: John Holt, president and CEO

Below left: The credit union's main office, located at 521 Cromwell Avenue in Rocky Hill

The Associated Construction Company

The Associated Construction Company is, first and foremost, the success story of a young immigrant boy, hailing from a small town in Northern Italy, who came to the United States to realize the American Dream.

Associated Construction Company Headquarters Building, 1010 Wethersfield Avenue, Hartford.

Arriving in Deep River, Connecticut at the age of 13 with his family, who was trying to escape the danger in Europe brought on by World War I, Angelo J.M. Giardini quickly adjusted to life in the land of opportunity. Graduating as valedictorian of his high school class, Giardini earned his bachelor's degree in civil engineering from Rensselaer Polytechnic Institute in Troy, NY in 1932. He then spent ten years honing his skills as a builder with two old-line contracting firms. It was in August, 1942 that Giardini set out to fulfill a lifelong dream and start his own business.

Giardini originally opened the doors of Associated in Groton, CT to take advantage of the military defense contracting needs of the U.S. Navy (where several of his buildings still stand today). However, Associated's shoreline location was far from ideal. "He kiddingly said that when he took out his protractor and drew a circle around Groton CT, half of his market was in Long Island Sound," remembers his son, Thomas M. Giardini, now the company's President. "He didn't have 360 degrees of land around him." Angelo thought it made more sense to move Associated to the capitol city of Hartford, where opportunities lay in both public and private sector work in both the city and its rapidly growing suburbs. In 1946, the offices of Associated moved to a farmhouse at 1010 Wethersfield Avenue, Hartford CT where the business still resides today, occupying an award-winning masonry office building which serves as the gateway to the South End of Hartford.

Hartford turned out to be the perfect choice for Giardini. Associated Construction's work can be seen throughout the area. The original Bradley Field Airport Terminal Building in Windsor Locks, The Hartford Steam Boiler Building at One State Street, Bushnell Towers and Plaza, the Criminal Court Building on Lafayette Street, the WVIT Channel 30 Digital Media Center near I-84 in West Hartford, and major office buildings on ESPN's campus in Bristol, CT are just a few of the many notable landmarks that Associated has constructed over the course of its 70 year history. In addition, the company has also built more than 3,500 units of multifamily housing, 40 sewage treatment plants and over 30 school projects.

The diversity of the foregoing projects reflects a commitment to Angelo Giardini's vision and the successful business model which has allowed Associated to flourish in an industry where many have failed. "My dad was a believer in diversification because, in any given year, you never knew what the construction requirements for the area and its industries would be," says Tom Giardini. "We've always been a general contractor from the beginning. While others may have started as trade contractors and then later grew to offer general contracting services, Associated provided general contracting and construction management services from its first day in business. The business model of diversification has worked well for us. It has allowed Associated to withstand the booms and busts of the construction industry and always come out with our head above water. With the experience of a good management team in place to pave the way we've been able to work our way through challenging times, maintain the company and keep our people employed," says Giardini.

An enduring reputation for quality workmanship has kept Associated on many firm's short lists for major projects. "The company has maintained the standards started by my dad back in 1942, and even though the business has become more sophisticated, we still go back to the principle of giving our client the highest quality project for a competitive price," Tom says. He goes on to state, "We've established a company with people who have many different areas of expertise and we've maintained the same level of quality for the past 70 years. We haven't changed. You have to earn your stripes every day." It's this pride in workmanship and commitment to quality that Associated's clients' have come to appreciate and which keeps the company successful.

These satisfied clients include such major corporations as ESPN, many of the United Technologies Companies (Hamilton Sundstrand, Sikorsky Aircraft, Pratt & Whitney), NBC Universal, Aetna Inc., Boehringer Ingelheim, The Hartford Financial Services Group, Saint Francis Hospital and Medical Center, Saint Raphael's Hospital and Yale University. Associated has performed hundreds of millions of dollars of construction work on many projects of varying size and scope for these clients. Indeed, there is no better testament to Associated's ability to deliver a quality product than this type of repeat business. With its integrated teams of seasoned professionals, bright young engineers and management personnel who are dedicated to providing personalized service and attention to any project, no matter how small, Associated has consistently delivered showpiece buildings and facilities for these clients, and will continue to do so for the foreseeable future.

As Associated Construction prepares to celebrate its 70th anniversary, it's not slowing down. The company will continue to hold firmly to its values and set higher benchmarks for performance in the construction industry. Indeed, Associated puts its name on the line with every construction project it builds. It understands that, unlike many other industries, its products remain in public view for many years to come and all to see. Clients have come to appreciate Associated's professional team of people that oversee the construction of well-built projects. They have learned to expect the Associated Construction Company difference, and that is what they receive with every project.

Above: ESPN Office and Broadcast Facility in Connecticut.

Left: One State Street, downtown Hartford Home of The Hartford Steam Boiler Inspection & Insurance Company, and The PolytechnicON20 Restaurant.

The Simon Konover Company

The Simon Konover Company: Still doing business on a handshake.

Early on, Simon Konover escaped the Holocaust, making his way to join his brother in the United States, working in the floor covering business. By 1957, Simon Konover was developing properties out of the trunk of his car. He drove from site to site, making deals on a handshake. He embarked on a mission of ownership, development and management of commercial real estate in the New England and New York marketplaces, focusing his efforts on neighborhood strip malls anchored by grocery stores.

After celebrating nearly 55 years in business, The Simon Konover Company has evolved into a nationally recognized, diverse real estate organization with offices in West Hartford, Connecticut and Deerfield Beach, Florida, says Jane Konover Coppa, company chief executive officer. Company leadership rests with its principals, Simon Konover, Coppa, his daughter — and his son, Steven Konover, together with their executive team. David Coppa, Simon's grandson, sits at the helm as CEO of Konover South. Despite its growth, the company remains family-owned and operated.

Over the past 55 years, The Simon Konover Company has built its reputation through integrity and creativity across the broad market sectors of hospitality, retail, multifamily, mixed use, specialty, office/industrial and construction industries. It has earned national recognition as an entrepreneurial organization and has established industry benchmarks for service and success. The firm's ability to serve many sectors has advanced its ability to help serve others. The Simon Konover Company, for example, is directly involved with Supportive Housing programs, a cost-effective combination of affordable housing and services that help people live stable, productive lives in their communities.

"Our diverse platform has given the Konover family a strategic grounding in its philanthropic mission through The Doris & Simon Konover Family Foundation — and of particular note — a very close relationship with Paul Newman's Hole in the Wall Gang group," says Jane Coppa. The company was the initial sponsor of the Annual Camp Challenge Ride which raises funds to help send children with illnesses to summer camp free of charge. In fact, Simon Konover worked with Paul Newman upon inception of the Camp in Ashford, Conn., and donated his services to help build the camp facilities.

The Simon Konover Company and its affiliated companies north and south now employ more than 700 associates in 10 states.

"We capitalize on organizational and employee strengths and acknowledge our associates as our greatest assets," Jane Coppa said. More than 50 of these team members operate from the company's West Hartford headquarters, including the executive team, with the help of supportive services, risk management, human resources, payroll and information technology departments. All help the firm maintain its success and act in the best interest of its clients and neighbors. The company's goal is to prosper through asset preservation and growth for the benefit of investors, partners and associates and to make meaningful contributions to the communities in which we live and do business, Jane Coppa explains. And the company's territory is broadening: it has developed, constructed, owned and managed an extensive portfolio of shopping centers, hotels, residential communities, office buildings, industrial facilities, mixed-use and specialty properties from Wisconsin to Florida to Massachusetts.

What does the future hold for this progressive company? Continued growth, said Coppa. "Our mission is to focus in areas where The Simon Konover Company can be 'best in class' as we navigate the future."

Top Right: One Century Tower located at 265 Church Street, New Haven.

Above: Simon Konover, Founder & Chairman, and Jane Konover Coppa, Principal & Chief Executive Officer

Suburban Companies Inc.

Suburban Companies Inc. Founded in 1968 by Glenn Pratt, the company has become a leader in the facilities services industry.

Left to right: Tom Teasdale, Consultant; Russ Stratton, General Manager; Jose Gonzalez, Operations Manager; Ivan Sarmiento, Operations Manager; Alvaro Mattos, Area Manager.

Suburban Companies
- Commercial Cleaning
- Carpet Cleaning
- Private School Services
- Building Services
- Construction
- Maintenance & Repairs
- Labor Support

From green cleaning concepts to the finest training and education at all personnel levels, Suburban Companies strives to exceed customer expectations. The business has grown exponentially since its first office opened in Braintree, Mass. In 1985, it established a home in Hartford, absorbing the former Janitor Services Inc. Today, the company has expanded to offer full facilities outsourcing services, making it the one-stop shop for commercial cleaning services and building maintenance.

Suburban Companies comprises two divisions: *Suburban Contract Cleaning* and *Suburban Building Services*. *Suburban Contract Cleaning* provides a variety of commercial cleaning services throughout the Northeast, Mid-Atlantic, and Mid-West, with operating offices located in Braintree, MA; Pawtucket, RI; and West Hartford, CT. Services include general office cleaning, floor maintenance and restoration, carpet cleaning, window cleaning, pest control, as well as other special service tasks.

Suburban Building Services offers construction, maintenance and repairs, and labor services to its commercial clients throughout New England. With a core group of technicians, tradesmen, carpenters, and laborers, *Suburban Building Services* works on projects of any size, from interior build-outs to painting and construction clean-ups. Its staff is trained to complete projects efficiently and deliver the highest quality service.

During the recent recession, Suburban Companies has worked diligently to retain its customer base while remaining price competitive in the ever-changing marketplace. Essential to this effort is a commitment to providing a better "value" to current and prospective clients — a concept that resonates in these tough economic times. The company has also seen more growth in associations with third-party management groups, which can lead to new client relationships, said Russ Stratton, Regional General Manager. "Creating job growth and opportunities for members of the local community is a priority for our company," he said.

What does the future hold for Suburban Companies? Diversification. "Providing a broader scope of facilities outsourcing services — [and] not just being recognized for commercial cleaning," said Stratton. "Suburban has already separated itself from the competition through its depth of management, broader scope of facility outsourcing services, superior service delivery, and fast customer response time," said Stratton. "We will further differentiate ourselves by constantly adding to our offering. When it comes to facility services, we want to do it all."

For more information, call (877) 778-1101 or visit www.suburbancompanies.com.

TRUMPF Inc.

The year was 1969. From man's first walk on the moon to the debut of the first home computer, it was a year marked with innovation, creativity and significant milestones in society — including the founding of Germany-based TRUMPF Group's U.S. subsidiary in Farmington, Connecticut.

Assembly line for the TruLaser 1030 laser cutting machine - designed and built in Farmington.

Established by Christian Trumpf in 1923 and headquartered in Ditzingen, Germany, TRUMPF is one of the world's largest manufacturers of sheet metal fabricating equipment and a world leader in industrial laser technology.

TRUMPF Inc., the second largest of the TRUMPF Group subsidiaries, owes its presence in North America to the pioneering spirit of an enterprising engineer, Berthold Leibinger, who obtained permission from Mr. Trumpf more than four decades ago to find an office in a country where the market was still untapped for TRUMPF machine tools.

After scouting out many of the major manufacturing hubs in the U. S., a weary Leibinger visited a friend in Connecticut on his way home to Germany. It was during this trip that he was introduced to the Farmington Industrial Park, which would become TRUMPF's American home and the company's North American headquarters.

It wasn't long before Leibinger's foresight and ingenuity led him to become president and managing partner of the TRUMPF Group. Today, Professor Leibinger and his family own TRUMPF. His daughter, Dr. Nicola Leibinger-Kammueller, is president and chairwoman of the managing board of this independent, privately held company.

Since its establishment in 1969, TRUMPF Inc. has grown from just three employees to 550 employees and is now the largest manufacturer of fabricating equipment and industrial lasers in the U.S. The company is the perfect example of Berthold Leibinger's theory: "To be truly successful in a country, you must be immersed in the culture and its mentality."

TRUMPF Inc. is the third-largest taxpayer in Farmington, and in spite of these turbulent economic times, during fiscal year 2010-2011 the company experienced its second most successful year in its history.

Innovation lies at the heart of TRUMPF's culture, and during a time when other companies were retreating from the marketplace, in the fourth quarter of 2009 TRUMPF Inc. launched a new, flagship product, the TruLaser 1030. Completely conceived, designed and built in Farmington, the TruLaser 1030 is an innovative sheet metal fabricating machine with great relevance to today's manufacturers. It has, in fact, revolutionized the industry.

Featuring TRUMPF technology at an affordable price, the TruLaser 1030 allows already-established fabricators to add laser cutting to their list of capabilities, and it also affords aspiring entrepreneurs the opportunity to launch a sheet metal fabricating business.

But the TruLaser 1030 is only one example of TRUMPF Inc.'s commitment to research and development initiatives, an area in which the company invests heavily. The TruLaser 1030 laser cutting system's options are empowering to fabricators, who can choose the model best suited for their unique business requirements. And one of those options is TRUMPF's TruCoax laser.

The TruCoax, a diffusion-cooled CO_2 laser, is state-of-the-art technology from Farmington. This laser is particularly impressive because of its light weight, small footprint, compact design, and low maintenance requirements.

However, TRUMPF's definition of success extends beyond products to include a strong commitment to contributing to the quality of life in its community. TRUMPF and its employees donate time and resources to many local and regional civic, social and charitable projects, including MetroHartford Alliance, Farmington Chamber of Commerce, Race for the Cure, Fidelco Guide Dog Foundation, Farmington Library, Connecticut Science Center, Greater Hartford Arts Council, the Hartford Symphony Orchestra, the German School of Connecticut, and other Connecticut-based organizations.

To help train the workforce of tomorrow, TRUMPF

Above: Aerial view of TRUMPF's North American Headquarters, Farmington.

Left: The TruLaser 1030 features high quality cutting of thin gauge materials.

has donated high-tech production equipment to local and regional educational institutions, awarded scholarships to future engineering students and contributed to projects with the Center for Next Generation Manufacturing, Connecticut Business & Industry Association, Connecticut Center for Advanced Technology, The School of Engineering and the University of Connecticut, Central Connecticut State University, Massachusetts Institute of Technology, Tunxis Community College, and Three Rivers Community College.

TRUMPF frequently welcomes local vocational schools and high schools to visit its production facilities and learn about laser technologies.

In spite of the recent economic recession and its lingering effects, the company continues to do its part to enrich the lives of not only those who work at TRUMPF, but of the wider community.

TRUMPF exports to 48 states and 24 countries, with 98 percent of its business done outside of Connecticut and 30 percent outside of the U.S. In the case of the TruLaser 1030, approximately 70 percent of TRUMPF's production is for overseas markets. TRUMPF considers itself fortunate to conduct business in a society that offers avenues for taking products to other areas of the globe where they can have a positive impact on quality of life.

While the future looks bright for TRUMPF, the company's ability to remain in Connecticut hinges in large part on support shown by the governing bodies responsible for creating regulations relevant to the state's manufacturers. TRUMPF firmly believes that it is in everyone's best interest to make American manufacturing more competitive and more productive.

UnitedHealth Group

UnitedHealth Group has been helping people live healthier lives for nearly four decades.

The company — originally called Charter Med Inc. — was founded in 1974 by a group of physicians seeking to expand health benefits coverage for consumers.

While the insurance industry and many of its largest companies are more than a century old, UnitedHealth Group has grown quickly in its comparatively young, 37-year span.

UnitedHealth Group has grown to become the largest health and well being company in the nation, serving more than 75 million people worldwide. Throughout its history, innovation has been the hallmark of UnitedHealth Group. The company introduced the nation's first network-based health plan for seniors in 1979; a national transplant network in 1989 that directs patients to high-quality physicians and facilities for complex medical needs; and electronic health care ID cards in 2003 to verify insurance eligibility within seconds. The company continues to be a trailblazer, using the latest consumer technology such as smartphones to empower customers by helping them become better informed health care consumers.

UnitedHealth Group is comprised of six businesses that operate under two distinct brands, UnitedHealthcare and Optum. UnitedHealthcare provides health benefits; access to physicians; and access to hospitals to more than 38 million individuals who are in employer-sponsored, Medicare and Medicaid programs. Optum provides information and technology-enabled health services to consumers, care providers, health systems and employers.

Minnesota-based UnitedHealth Group now has more than 87,000 employees across the country, including 4,000 in Connecticut. Company operations grew most notably in Connecticut with the 1995 acquisition of The MetraHealth Companies, the group health care operations of Travelers Insurance Co. and Metropolitan Life Insurance Co. The acquisition allowed UnitedHealth Group to become a leader in serving health benefits programs for large, multinational corporations, and Hartford remains home to the company's national accounts business.

In fact, last year UnitedHealth Group deepened its commitment to the Hartford region by investing $35 million to renovate the landmark CityPlace building and moving more than 2,000 employees into the facility, now known as UnitedHealthcare Center. UnitedHealth Group's Connecticut operations are among the company's largest.

UnitedHealth Group and its employees are also dedicated to serving their communities, contributing time, talents and other resources to support not-for-profit organizations and activities. Last year, 77 percent of UnitedHealth Group's employees across the nation performed community volunteer work totaling more than 200,000 hours and donated $14 million, including company-matching funds, to good causes.

The commitment and passion of the company's employees is likely one of the biggest reasons Fortune magazine named UnitedHealth Group the Most Admired Company in the insurance and managed-care industry this year.

At UnitedHealth Group, employees' passion to make a difference where they live and work is an inspiration that drives the company's mission — helping people live healthier lives and make U.S. health care work better. The company is proud of the work its Connecticut employees do to achieve UnitedHealth Group's national leadership status in health care.

Our employees regularly give their time to help promote healthier lives in the Hartford communities. In May, UnitedHealth Group volunteers expanded the Battles Street Community Garden, enabling nearly 40 families in Hartford's Clay Arsenal neighborhood to grow healthy, fresh produce. (From left to right) Matthew Perry, Matthew Poulin, Celoris Allen and Amanda Hill.

UnitedHealth Group invested $35 million renovating CityPlace — now known as UnitedHealthcare Center — in downtown Hartford. The project included recycling more than 247 tons of materials to build a modern, environmentally friendly facility for its 2,100 employees.

UnitedHealth Group employees are proud to donate their time, skills and money to a number of local organizations that help create a vibrant community throughout the Hartford region, including:

Foodshare	Boys and Girls Club	Greater Hartford Arts Council	South Park Inn
American Cancer Society	Connecticut Science Center	Make-A-Wish	The Knox Parks Foundation
American Heart Association	Hartford Marathon Foundation	MetroHartford Alliance	United Way
American Red Cross	The Governor's Prevention Partnership	ProBono Partnership	YMCA

Horton International LLC

Horton International LLC maintains a strong commitment to Connecticut's businesses and industries while continuing to expand its U.S. and global presence.

Horton International LLC is a global retained executive search firm serving a wide range of clients in Connecticut, the U.S. and worldwide. Partners Larry Brown and Bob Gilchrist run the U.S. operations from their headquarters in West Hartford and serve as board members of Horton Group International Limited, the firm's governing body, based in the U.K.

With the advantage of over 40 locations spread throughout Europe, Asia, Latin America and Australia, Horton International is well positioned to meet its domestic clients' growing demand for executive talent with global expertise. Despite expansion overseas, the firm's commitment to Connecticut businesses and industries remains strong.

"Everyone wants to expand into emerging markets and there's a dearth of talent that can operate linguistically and culturally in other parts of the world," says Gilchrist. "There's a significant need for global talent to serve the global marketplace."

Horton International has a strong U.S. presence with branch operations in Boston, New York, Philadelphia and Charlotte, N.C. Its client base ranges from Fortune 100 corporations to mid-market companies and start-up businesses that retain Horton International to recruit board-level and executive talent in functional areas including general management, finance, human resources, marketing, manufacturing and engineering.

The Horton International team of 10 brings a wealth of industry experience and a high level of professionalism to the search process, enjoying a well-earned reputation for building strong and enduring partnerships with clients. All Horton International search consultants are seasoned professionals with prior successful business careers in diverse industries including financial services, life sciences, technology and manufacturing, enabling them to quickly and realistically assess organizational needs of client companies. Horton International is large enough to provide the necessary resources and expertise to meet U.S. and global recruiting needs while maintaining the intimacy of a small firm with a commitment to personal attention and client service.

As a retained executive search firm, Horton International provides objective advice on all candidates, internal and external, as its fee is not contingent on hiring a specific individual. Horton International provides value to both clients and candidates by presenting only the most qualified candidates based on an accurate and comprehensive assessment of a candidate's experience and organizational fit.

Horton International conducts extensive research to identify the best talent, and through comprehensive assessment, narrows the field to top candidates with the best prospects for success. "Technology has substantially changed the way potential candidates can be identified, but it has not changed in the critical issue of the selection and assessment of the right candidate for the client," observes Gilchrist. "Technology allows you now more than ever to access active candidates. But there are a lot of people who are 'passive' candidates — head down, working hard, doing their jobs and not actively looking. Reaching them and getting them engaged is something technology can't get you — it has to be the interpersonal connection."

(Left to right) Bob Gilchrist and Larry Brown, Managing Partners, Horton International.

Stockton Associates

*For the last 30 years, Ed Stockton's passion for Connecticut has taken the form of **Stockton Associates**, which specializes in the use of economic analysis for the solution of real estate problems and opportunities.*

Above: Marilyn and Ed Stockton at their Bloomfield office.

As Commissioner of Economic Development for Connecticut for six and a half years, Ed Stockton made a career out of promoting the state as a great place to live and work. Stockton has never stopped believing that "there is no place like Connecticut." With a team of individuals with diverse capabilities, including his wife and business partner, Marilyn Stockton, Stockton Associates utilizes "unique capabilities rooted in economic expertise and international experience" to assist a variety of clients.

Ed Stockton's knowledge, understanding and experience with local, state and federal government, combined with Marilyn's background in real estate, education and graphic arts, serve as a remarkable resource for clients. The Stockton's shared love of traveling, coupled with their devotion to the state of Connecticut, has helped to establish Stockton Associates' niche in the international market. This consulting firm has corporate investor contacts throughout the world, and specializes in finding development opportunities for overseas companies in the United States. "Connecticut is extremely attractive to overseas companies," says Ed. "The state is known for being a leader in advanced technology and possesses a highly skilled work force from which these companies can draw." Those who do come to Connecticut are attracted to its "sophisticated population." Connecticut, according to Stockton, really is a "unique and vibrant" place to live and work and international clients are excited for the opportunity to partake in this environment.

E/CONNomics, an economic consulting firm specializing in the analysis of the Connecticut economy, is also closely linked to Stockton Associates. Equipped with an extensive database, the company is capable of covering all aspects of statewide economic activity. With detailed information on labor force, personal income, wage rates, local taxes and more, the company can assist others in successful stratagems to "maximize opportunities and minimize problems." This information has proved priceless to companies within the region and abroad.

Over the years Ed Stockton has been applauded for his efforts in both government and trade. Most recently he was awarded the Todd Ouida World Trade Award for exemplifying the Connecticut World Trade Association's "objective of peace and stability through trade." Despite the accolades Ed has received over the years, he remains most proud of bringing in and creating more jobs for the citizens of Connecticut. Assisting international companies — such as Lego, Trumpf and Konica — set up in the state, as well as helping companies within the state find an international market in which to export their product, gives the Stocktons and those they work with a sense of a job well done.

LAZ Parking

Formed in 1981 as a valet parking company servicing restaurants in Hartford and Boston, LAZ Parking has developed into one of the fastest growing parking companies in the United States.

Above: From left to right is the LAZ Parking Shareholder's Group. Front row: Robert DeBurro, David Lerman, Michael Kuziak, Alan Lazowski, Andrew Tuchler, Marc Lutwack, Jeff Karp, Kynn Knight. Back row: Michael Harth, Ray Skoglund, Nathan Owen, Jim Marzi

Below: Members of the LAZ Team are joined by Special Olympic Staff and Athletes at the 2011 LAZ Charitable Foundation Golf Tournament

Operating 1,349 parking facilities in 21 states and 235 cities and towns, the company manages 503,391 parking spaces, 5,700 employees, and $508 million in parking receipts.

Alan Lazowski, founder and CEO, built LAZ Parking in a unique and enviable manner — he teamed up with his two best friends and went into the parking business. Friends since middle school in Bloomfield, Lazowski, Jeff Karp and Michael Harth were trying to figure out a way to make money during college, work together and be their own bosses. Lazowski started valet parking cars in Hartford, Harth got going in Southern California, and Karp started valet parking in Boston. The rest — as they say — is history.

It was slow and steady growth for many years, until 1992, when LAZ began its expansion out of New England with the opening of a regional office in Atlanta. Today the company has regional offices in Hartford, Boston, New York, Atlanta, Philadelphia, Washington D.C., Miami, Chicago, Dallas, Houston, San Francisco, Los Angeles and San Diego.

Early in 2007, LAZ Parking partnered with Morgan Stanley to become the operating partner of the largest underground parking operation in the United States — Chicago Downtown Parking System — encompassing 9,200 parking spaces at Millennium Park.

Later that year, LAZ announced the formation of LAZ Parking Realty Investors with an initial equity commitment of $200 million from a major investment firm. The investment vehicle represented a new joint venture parking fund that leveraged the LAZ operating portfolio and provided LAZ with the ability to greatly expand its acquisitions of parking real estate across the country. "The formation of LAZ Parking Realty Investors LLC represents an opportunity to leverage our core competency of maximizing parking cash flow into broader and more incentive fee ownership positions," Lazowski said.

"We are looking at opportunities which include privatization of municipal parking systems, acquisition of condominium and stand-alone garages, as well as urban land purchases throughout the United States."

In the fall of 2007, LAZ Parking formed a partnership with the largest parking operator in the world, VINCI Park, headquartered in Paris, France. The transaction represented a mutual growth strategy by both parking leaders. VINCI Park built an extremely successful network of parking operations in countries throughout Western and Eastern Europe and Canada involving 1.3 million parking spaces in 1,800 locations across 16 countries. As part of the joint venture, LAZ Parking can support VINCI Park's growth by providing top-quality management backed by a successful track record of significant growth.

LAZ's corporate culture is unique in that the founders of the company have created a family environment — no easy task when the company has grown to 5,700 employees. Michael Kuziak, chief operating officer, joined Lazowski shortly after the company's formation in 1981. He attributes the company's success to a true sense of caring about all employees. "Being able to hire someone at an hourly rate and move them up the ladder through mentorship, coaching and training so that

Above: LAZ Regional VP's and General Managers lift LAZ Founder and CEO Alan Lazowski.

Left: LAZ Parking Customer Service at its best at LAZFly Airport Parking at Bradley International Airport.

they can join the ranks of senior management is extremely rewarding to witness," said Kuziak. He has overseen rapid expansion during the past few years and knows firsthand the importance of everyone working together to build a reputation based on honesty, integrity and plain hard work.

In 2010, LAZ extended these values to the communities it serves, in the midst of a weak economy. "Now is exactly the right time to establish a charitable foundation, because the need in our communities is greater than ever," said Michael Harth, president of the West Coast region of Sunset/LAZ Parking. The foundation's mission is to contribute time and financial resources to charitable organizations that make a positive difference in people's lives. In order to involve as many LAZ employees as possible, the company launched a contest asking all employees to nominate a national charity. Special Olympics was ultimately selected to receive financial and volunteer support during the first few years of the foundation's activities.

As the company moves forward, major investments in human resources, accounting infrastructure and IT are underway. While LAZ manages virtually every type of parking operation — hotels, stadium and event parking, residential projects, office buildings, mixed-use developments, shuttle services, transportation hubs, municipalities, valet services and hospitals — dedicated divisions for medical, hotels, and government services have been established. LAZ also offers consulting in revenue control equipment, audit controls, traffic flow, design and layout optimization and parking enforcement.

LAZ's modern success adheres to the same principles that guided its early years. When LAZ was provided the opportunity to manage its first garage, a 600-space facility for the Hilton Hotel, net income was increased by 50 percent in the first 12 months. "There was no real magic to what we did. We were young, aggressive, honest valet parkers who focused on the facility's financial performance and service requirements," says Lazowski. Today, he said, that same story resonates in each facility the firm acquires and increased profitability and enhanced customer service result. "We have skillfully built a reputation based on efficiency, integrity — and above all - creating opportunities for our employees and value for our clients," Lazowski said.

The Governor's Prevention Partnership

With a focus on Connecticut's youth, The Governor's Prevention Partnership is a statewide public-private alliance, building a strong, future workforce through mentoring, prevention of school violence, bullying, underage drinking, alcohol and substance abuse.

Above: Governor Malloy (center) with Logan West, Connecticut's Outstanding Teen 2010, who was bullied in middle school (left) and Talan Daigle, a student mentored by Patty Murphy, a vice president at Webster Bank (not pictured here).

*Right: Governor Malloy thanks The Partnership's Partners In Prevention: (left to right) **Alan Must**, VP, State Government and Legislative Affairs, Purdue Pharma; **David Fusco**, President, Anthem Blue Cross and Blue Shield; **Katie Wade**, VP State Government Affairs, CIGNA; **Don Langer**, Plan President, CEO of AmeriChoice of CT; **Peg Parks**, Human Resources, LEGO; **Peter Holland**, Director, State Government Affairs, UTC; **Governor Dannel Malloy**; **Tim Bannon**, Chief of Staff, Office of the Governor; **Marlene Ibsen**, President, Travelers Foundation; **Mark Bertolini**, Chairman, CEO and President, AETNA; **Jill Spineti**, President, The Governor's Prevention Partnership; **Jeffrey Brown**, Executive VP, Chief Administrative Officer, Webster Bank.*

"No doubt, children are our most precious resource," said Governor Dannel Malloy addressing a group of top business leaders in May 2011. "We must make every effort, despite the times, to preserve their health and well-being, and ensure a successful future for every child in Connecticut."

Malloy is co-chair of The Governor's Prevention Partnership, a public-private partnership launched in 1989 to stem the rising tide of substance abuse. Don Langer, CEO of AmeriChoice of Connecticut is co-chair of The Partnership representing the private sector. "The Governor's Prevention Partnership aligns with our mission to engage in community service projects that benefit those with the greatest need and to provide children and families with an opportunity to build strong, healthy futures," Langer said.

In its early years, The Partnership was instrumental in helping Connecticut corporations establish drug-screening policies and develop addiction recovery programs for employees. Over time it became clear that problems with substance abuse may begin as early as childhood and adolescence, well before an individual enters the workforce. For this reason, The Partnership in recent years has expanded its mission to include early intervention, with the goal of impacting tomorrow's workforce. "We've remained vigilant in identifying issues affecting youth ... and open to the fact that at different moments in time, different issues must take the lead," said Jill Spineti, Partnership President and CEO.

The Governor's Prevention Partnership attacks the problem of substance abuse from all sides. "We work with parents and educators to be the first line of defense," said Spineti. "With parents it's about how to talk to their kids, warning signs to look for, which drugs — including prescription drugs — are popular, how to give their children skills to refuse drugs. At the schools, we work with superintendents and teachers to ensure that students get the right information."

Since alcohol is the most commonly abused substance by school-age children, with nearly 50% of youth reporting that downing five or more alcoholic drinks nearly everyday is "no big deal" (2010 Parent Attitude Tracking Survey), much of The Partnership's focus has been on cutting off supply. When the program was initiated, 75% of the merchants were selling to minors. Now, after years of enforcement and education, less than 18% of licensed outlets are selling alcohol to underage customers. The Partnership collaborates with local coalitions to develop and implement comprehensive, community-specific strategies that reinforce the drug prevention message. There are 32 coalitions operating across the state. The Partnership's efforts have been successful: the number of underage students who reported consuming alcohol in the last 30 days dropped 8.9%.

The Partnership has been instrumental in influencing legislation that strengthens underage drinking laws related to 'social hosting,' making it illegal for youth to possess alcohol on private property and penalizing adults who permit underage drinking. An upcoming challenge will be the development of a new strategy following the changes to marijuana laws that decriminalize possession of small amounts of the substance — less than half an ounce.

A key collaborator in the fight against substance abuse is law enforcement, and The Partnership's training programs for police have been instrumental in curbing underage drinking. "We work with law enforcement to provide resources and information to help them safely disperse house parties, conduct sales to minors compliance checks and identify current trends and other best practices. Our law enforcement conferences sell out every year," said Spineti.

Partnership teams work closely with educators to identify at-risk children and help them resolve problems that make them susceptible to substance abuse. Bullying has surfaced as a major factor impacting youth well-being and success. One in four high school children report naving been bullied in the past year (2009 School Survey). This led The Partnership to advocate on behalf of victims to enact stronger anti-bullying legislation. New cyber-bullying legislation permits school officials to step in when school-age children are victims. Former bullying victim Logan West, Connecticut's Outstanding Teen 2010, works closely with The Partnership, educating the media, state legislators and school officials on the need for anti-bullying policies, and empowering other victims of school bullying.

Through its Connecticut Mentoring Partnership, a statewide support network for mentoring, local mentoring programs are strengthened. More than 190,000 children in Connecticut have life situations that place them at risk for personal and academic failure. These risk factors include poverty, inadequate early childhood experiences. However, children who have ongoing relationships with caring adults are more likely to avoid alcohol or other drugs, stay in school and get good grades, have a better self-image and have better relationships with their families and friends.

Hundreds of Connecticut corporations have enabled their employees to join more than 9,000 adults to become mentors to 12,000 at-risk students. "The CT Mentoring Partnership incorporates attention to all of the youth issues we represent; our goal is to foster success of today's youth so they are ready to take their place in the workforce," said Spineti. "Any child who is bullied, on drugs or involved in underage drinking would certainly benefit from the support and guidance of a mentor. A mentor has the power to improve a child's life."

A shining example of corporate involvement is Webster Bank, a company that encourages employees to participate by allowing them time to volunteer. The bank sponsors more than 100 employees in 30 towns across the state. Patty Murphy, a vice president at Webster Bank has mentored Talan Daigle for six years, offering him much needed support and encouragement. Her investment of time and attention has paid off, and Talan has turned his life around both in school and at home. Many more mentors, especially men and minorities, are needed.

Connecticut's business community has a longstanding commitment to prevention. As deep budget cuts have reduced or eliminated many services provided by non-profit organizations, it is noteworthy that this program's budget has remained intact, further demonstrating the value of a public-private partnership. "Without the leadership of our co-chairs Governor Malloy and Don Langer, and support from our Board and generous corporate and community partners, the Governor's Prevention Partnership would not be able to continue its vital mission," said Spineti.

Governor Malloy, Co-Chair of The Governor's Prevention Partnership and Jill Spineti, President of The Partnership, surrounded by the young people The Partnership so passionately serves.

Carousel Industries

Carousel Industries is one of the truly outstanding business success stories in Connecticut over the past two decades.

Beginning in 1992 as an idea in the minds of two entrepreneurs, the company today is a nationally respected technology integrator for voice, video and data with an enviable customer list that includes Bank of America, Travelers, Revlon and CBS. Carousel Industries has experienced average sales growth of 30 to 50 percent since it was founded, and is on track this year to generate $300 million in revenues. The company's story of dramatic growth clearly demonstrates that the entrepreneurial spirit is alive and well in Connecticut.

Based in New England with 1,000 employees nationwide, Carousel's sales headquarters in Windsor is home to 100 employees and the company recently annexed additional office space to accommodate another 60. During a time of prolonged economic stagnation and less-than-stellar job creation, the company added 200 employees last year and has 150 open job requisitions. Carousel has been honored numerous times as an Inc. 500 fast growth company and is a member of the Inc. 5000 fastest-growing businesses in the last 20 years.

As the company approaches its 20th anniversary, a look back offers proof that a change in circumstances can be a blessing in disguise. Jeff Gardner, Carousel's CEO, was working in public accounting in Connecticut in 1992. "I had the entrepreneurial bug and wanted to get out of my day job," said Gardner. The opportunity came unexpectedly when his brother-in-law Mike Vickers was laid off from his position with an engineering firm. One of Vickers' customers kept calling him about a computer-cabling contract. He talked it over with Gardner, who said, "Why don't we go ahead and do the work?"

They launched Carousel Industries, and with the profits from the job, the two decided to buy a sandwich shop in Rhode Island, naming it Carousel Marketplace. "We had a great first year. We did somewhere between $500,000 and $600,000 in sandwiches," Gardner said. Meanwhile, calls kept coming in for cabling jobs. "We had one phone line," he said. "We answered the phone: 'Carousel' and it would be 'I need two Italian grinders, two ham and a tuna,' or 'Hello Carousel, I need a quote for 2,500 feet of fiber optic cable.'" By this time, Gardner's cousin Eric had joined on as the first employee.

The cabling business grew, and over the next few years, sales began to outpace the sandwich shop. The growth came from one client who liked the job they were doing so well that they kept giving them more business. Reynolds & Reynolds, a leading provider of automotive retailing solutions for car dealers and automakers, hired Carousel Industries to wire all of its Rhode Island dealerships, then all of New England and eventually the entire East Coast. By this time Carousel was getting frequent requests from customers for help with their phone systems. In 1997, the company applied to become a Lucent Technologies (now Avaya) reseller to accommodate these requests and pave the way for continued growth.

The next major pivot point in Carousel's history came in 2001, when Jim Marsh joined the company as a partner. "Jim had a lot of very large customers, and we were primarily doing car dealerships," said Gardner. Before Marsh came on board, the company's capabilities were narrow in scope, but Marsh quickly changed that. "Carousel was not authorized or certified in any real enterprise-type communication product, so that was part of the process, to build resources and get certified or authorized to sell to large global accounts," said Marsh. Today Carousel partners with more than 30 of the top technology companies in the world and offers customers a comprehensive menu of fully integrated solutions.

Marsh established Carousel's sales headquarters in Connecticut, where the company already had a strong presence. He developed a training program similar to

James R. Marsh III, Senior Vice President of Carousel Industries.

baseball's farm team system, building the sales organization from the ground up, hiring recent college graduates. New recruits generate leads and over time graduate to outside sales. "Today we have about 75 guys that are on that farm team and outside we have about 140," said Marsh. Carousel is expanding aggressively both organically and through acquisitions, and the model provides a steady supply of trained sales professionals to launch and staff new offices across the country.

Carousel's acquisition strategy is two-pronged: to expand its footprint geographically, and to add new products and capabilities. The company has 28 regional locations nationwide and is expanding internationally to better serve global customers. Carousel offers more than 60 products, including unified communications, virtualization, video/collaboration, global networking, security, wireless infrastructure and dozens more.

A major concern of many large enterprises is the need to consolidate IT purchasing. "We have a Fortune 100 company and the customer said, 'I have 300 vendors that I purchase from on an annual basis and that's too many,'" explained Marsh. "We're able to be that one-stop solution that can do your consulting, your design, your implementation, your managed services and really be your IT help desk." One of the most effective ways Carousel has helped customers is by leveraging technology they already own. "When we do a needs analysis, we may learn that they have technology that is able to solve their business problems but is underutilized," said Marsh. "We redevelop, reprogram that technology to fix the problem."

Carousel Industries has achieved impressive success by listening to its customers and delivering results. "We find ways to drive efficiencies in and costs out," said Gardner. Carousel's goal is to become the trusted advisor for all technology solutions. "When customers small or large have some kind of technology challenge, or are doing an acquisition, or are looking at a five-year road map for their business and need some expertise from a technical perspective, we want them to pick up the phone and call Carousel."

Above: Members of the executive sales training program at Carousel along with two of the program's directors, far left: Paul Millette, far right: Robert Linder, and the program founder, James R. Marsh III, in the center.

Left: Carousel's mission statement is displayed in every office from coast to coast, reinforcing their commitment to their customers and employees.

Charles Wareham and Associates / LPL Financial

For state of the art advice on paying for college, check out this boutique financial firm. When it comes to the college funding to retirement transition, nobody does it better than Wareham & Associates!

One of the major milestones of parenthood is sending a child off to college for the first time. For the average family, this triumphant moment is often overshadowed by a sense of panic as sticker shock sets in. How do they pay for college and still have enough left over for retirement?

Many Connecticut families have turned to Charles Wareham and Associates - a full service financial planning firm which also happens to specialize in college planning. "Easily 85 percent of my clientele comes from families who have a senior in high school, and they are in a full-on panic mode about how they're going to pay for college," said Wareham. "So we help them through that process and then shift gears to help do damage control for their retirement." The process is a long term one - typically 15-20 years of working together to achieve financial independence. "We are one of the only firms in the state that understands the college funding to retirement piece really well," added Wareham.

The firm has relationships with over 45 high schools in Connecticut where they conduct the financial aid night presentation for parents. This "How to Pay for College" program covers not only financial aid, college savings, and loan strategies, but also creative ways to pay for college. Each September Wareham also hosts a luncheon at The Hartford Club for guidance professionals to update them on trends and opportunities in the college funding environment. The event is the only one of its kind in the state being conducted by a licensed financial professional, according to Wareham.

"The most effective way to invest for college and retirement is: "Try not to lose money," said Wareham of the firm's investment philosophy. His goal is to design portfolios that tend to make money when times are good, and protect it when times are not.

Wareham and Associates is affiliated with LPL Financial, the nation's largest independent broker-dealer. The relationship allows the firm to offer an essentially unlimited selection of investment and financial planning solutions. "We can pick and choose from the full spectrum of investments and programs to custom-tailor what we do for our clients," Wareham explained.

Wareham's focus on college planning has proven to be a winning formula. Wareham and Associates has been named one of the top 25 fastest-growing companies by the Hartford Business Journal. The firm recently added several new advisors and expects to continue to add staff and expand.

The firm's offices at 750 Main Street in downtown Hartford give clients easy access to the group. And for Wareham, living and working in Hartford is surprisingly the culmination of a dream. While some might question the choice to relocate to Hartford, Charles - a native of Pennsylvania and Penn State graduate - chose Hartford as his home after college. "It had everything I was looking for - mountains, ocean, city, country, winter, summer, history, culture", Charles says. The city has made great strides, in his view. "The fact that there is energy and life on the street after 5 o'clock is huge," he said, enumerating positive changes that have taken root in recent years. Wareham believes in, and supports the vision of making Hartford a vibrant place for residents, workers and visitors. He is actively involved in his residential association, is a donor and supporter of First Night Hartford, a photographer for The Greater Hartford Festival of Jazz, and a member of Business for Downtown Hartford. "We're here because we believe in this city" he says.

Above: From left to right, advisors and staff Charles Wareham, Josh Orbach, Craig Breitsprecher, Barbara Mach.

Below: Advisor Charles Wareham delivers a presentation at Northwest Catholic High School.

HARTFORD BUSINESS JOURNAL

Hartford Business Journal has been helping people connect and grow their business throughout Greater Hartford and Connecticut for over 20 years.

Above: Gail Lebert, publisher, congratulates the winners at HBJ's annual Women in Business Awards.

Below: The CT Business Expo show floor is a great place to meet business people from across the state.

Business is not for the faint of heart. The business world is fast paced. The business world is analytical. The business world is built on relationships. The business world is demanding, and entertaining and very rewarding. Every business day, the team at the Hartford Business Journal is thinking about business. But not just the world of business — they are thinking about the business of Greater Hartford.

Since 1992, the Hartford Business Journal has informed readers about business news and information. Back then, the news was about the Hartford Whalers, insurance companies laying off workers in the midst of hard economic times, and G Fox closing the downtown Hartford location. Today Hartford Business Journal is a trusted source for news and information for the business community to track modern trends and stay one step ahead of the competition. And HBJ efforts haven't gone unrecognized. In 2011 the Alliance of Area Business Publications awarded the Hartford Business Journal two national awards: one for breaking news and one for HBJ's summer series, Road to Recovery.

In addition to the weekly newspaper, news is posted on HartfordBusiness.com throughout the day, keeping readers up to date. Website and daily newsletter readership numbers have exploded over the past three years. More than 60 percent of all HBJ readers, according to a recent independent survey, read both print and online versions of the news.

Hartford Business Journal continues to widen its scope of offerings, hosting award ceremonies and educational events to reach out to business leaders even more. Health Care Heroes, 40 Under Forty, Best Places to Work in CT, Women in Business, CFO of the Year, Business Champions, Energy Summit, eMarketing and Technology, and Lifetime Achievement Awards each have a following of people who want to meet each other, learn from each other and celebrate successes together.

Hartford Business Journal purchased a new event component, the CT Business EXPO, in 2008. This statewide business-to-business show has been a part of the community since 2000. "The CT Business Expo has been an important part of our own marketing to the business community. As the premier business publication, we know all of the issues about doing business in our region," said Joe Zwiebel, HBJ founding publisher. "We want to help people connect and grow their business — and the CT Business Expo is the perfect place for that to happen."

Giving back to the business community that it serves is a paramount priority of HBJ. "Over the years we have tried to be as generous as possible to support the non-profit community," said Gail Lebert, publisher of the Hartford Business Journal. "We recognize that they are businesses that often need an extra helping hand." Hartford Business Journal has supported the YMCA, United Way, Easter Seals, American Heart Association, HARC, Big Brothers/Big Sisters, Advertising Club of CT, American Marketing Association, CT Tech Council, FoodShare and many other groups through sponsorships, advertising and volunteering."

New England Business Media — a private company owned by Zwiebel and CEO Peter Stanton — is the parent company of Hartford Business Journal. New England Business Media also owns Worcester Business Journal, MetroWest495 Biz, and MAINEBIZ, in Portland, Maine. "Often people say, 'Are you in the newspaper business?' I remind them that we are in the business of providing our customers with high-value opportunities to connect with and sell their products and services to business decision makers," said Stanton. "Making these connections between our customers and their best prospects is the core of our business."

PHOTOGRAPHIC MOMENTS 191

Oakleaf Waste Management

Oakleaf Waste Management was founded in 1995 as a visionary company, evolving over the past 16 years into a 450-person team, serving many of the leading corporations in North America.

Oakleaf's continued growth is attributed to its first-to-market, asset-light business model, extensive vendor network and progressive methods of landfill diversion, asset recovery, improved recycling programming and environmental stewardship for clients.

2011 has been a remarkable year for Oakleaf in every capacity. On January 25, Oakleaf celebrated the grand opening of its new headquarters. More than 300 Oakleaf employees, vendors and dignitaries braved the cold for an opening celebration to support the relocation. The previous headquarters in East Hartford served the company well for a period of transition, but future business development and operational efficiencies were limited. Oakleaf's expansion and subsequent new headquarters at 415 Day Hill Road in Windsor has dramatically improved both client service and internal processes.

The headquarters are bright and open by design with plenty of natural light to create a dynamic work environment. Collaboration tables and multipurpose boardrooms for impromptu brainstorming are sprinkled throughout. White boards located throughout multiple hallways and plenty of meeting spaces help foster an efficient team atmosphere.

In keeping with Oakleaf's 'sustainability first' DNA, scores of green building elements were incorporated into the building's overall redesign. Carpet, ceramic tile and cafeteria counter tops were constructed using recycled materials. Remanufactured workstations were installed, preventing 250,000 lbs. of material from being sent to a landfill. The fitness area features a unique ceramic tile composed of 40 percent recycled content. The break area surfaces are locally manufactured in Baltimore, Maryland from 34 percent recycled post-industrial waste. The floors are constructed of natural cork.

Other sustainable elements include low VOC carpeting, Benjamin Aura GREENGUARD paint, energy recovery units in the basement and energy efficient

Grand opening celebration of Oakleaf's new headquarters at 415 Day Hill Road, Windsor:

From left to right: Town of Windsor Mayor – Donald Trinks, Oakleaf CEO Steve Preston, MetroHartford Alliance President and CEO – Oz Griebel.

Oakleaf CEO Steve Preston.

Town of Windsor Mayor – Donald Trinks.

fixtures. Additionally, 100 percent recyclable flooring, which emits no volatile organic compounds or VOCs is used in the lobby.

Even the majority of the art spread throughout Oakleaf is sustainably created. Oakleaf would like to issue a special thanks to Katrina, from the Greater Hartford Academy of Arts for loaning us her work of art for the new office. The piece is titled Book of Porcupines and it was created from recycled material!

Along with the new philosophy, came a renewed focus on the Oakleaf team and its core values. Oakleaf created the largest team ever to participate in Bike MS Steelcase Ride in Windsor on June 5th. Oakleaf's 100 participants raised over $19,000 in support of the local MS chapter.

The biggest news of 2011 was announced on July 28, 2011, when Waste Management acquired Oakleaf. The surprising and exciting news was supported with the tagline — Together, We Are Better. The acquisition greatly improves the service and product offerings for both organizations. Oakleaf shares Waste Management's strategic focus on sustainability, technological innovation and increased development of national accounts.

Oakleaf substantially increases Waste Management's client base while furthering its ability to provide comprehensive, best-in-class environmental solutions. Additionally, Oakleaf's vendor-hauler network expands Waste Management's service footprint to new geographies and offers customers turnkey shopping for environmental solutions.

Waste Management's client roster will also provide Oakleaf's vendors with expanded business opportunities. Post-collection services increase the scope for the vendor hauler network - which generates significant benefits for Waste Management and the network of vendors.

Oakleaf is proud to join Waste Management because it will enhance service offerings to clients resulting in improved sustainability, environmental stewardship and a positive impact on a larger community.

A bit about Waste Management: Waste Management (WM) is a $12.5 billion dollar company based in Houston, Texas. It is the leading provider of comprehensive waste management services in North America. Through its subsidiaries, the company provides collection, transfer, recycling, resource recovery and disposal services. It is the largest residential recycler, managing more than 8.5 million tons per year of material. That's enough to fill the Empire State Building 14.5 times. WM is also a leading developer, operator and owner of waste-to-energy and landfill gas-to-energy facilities in the United States. In fact, WM produces more renewable energy than the entire solar industry in the U.S. and creates enough energy to power more than 1 million homes. To date, WM landfills provide more than 26,000 acres of protected habitat for wildlife and 103 WM landfills and facilities are certified by the Wildlife Habitat Council. WM is also working to green the fleet. Currently, Waste Management operates more than 1000 alternative energy vehicles, like those powered by CNG. Today, more than 20 million customers rely on Waste Management.

Above: The new headquarters corresponds with Oakleaf's philosophy of bringing sophisticated, smart solutions to the Waste Industry.

Below: Oakleaf also volunteers and contributes to FOODSHARE – an organization at the heart of Greater Hartford's fight against hunger.

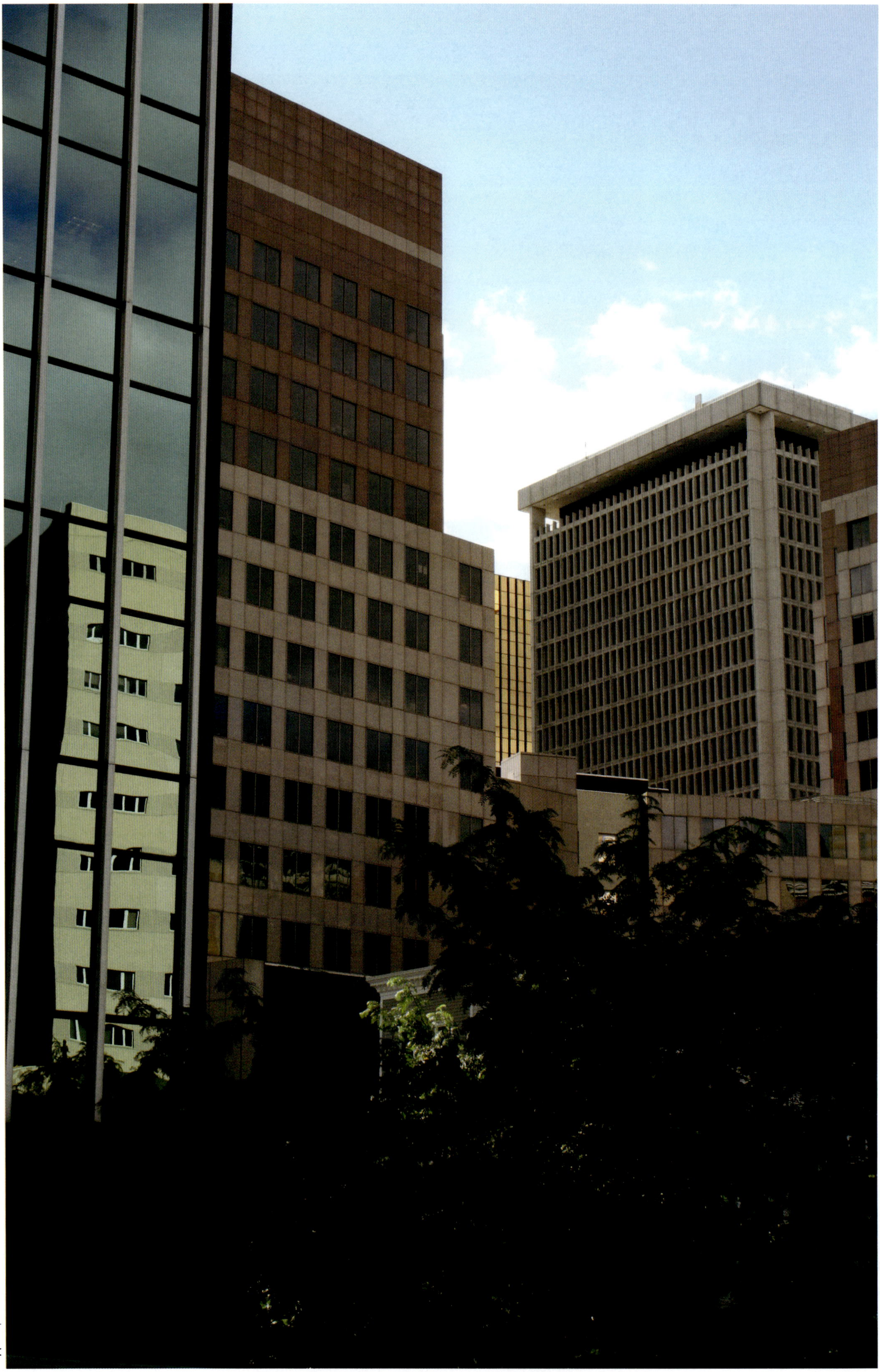

Lynn Mika

Cox Business

Cox Business provides voice, data, and video services for nearly 260,000 small and regional businesses, including healthcare providers, grades K-12 and higher education, financial institutions, and federal, state and local government organizations.

Seated L to R: John Crouse, Yvette Collins, Lorne Roux
Standing L to R: Brian Schulz, Suzette Roberts, Kerrie Salmon, Kim Procaccini, Denene Thompson, Doug Barber

Currently the seventh largest voice service provider in the United States, Cox Business supports more than 730,000 business phone lines nationwide. In New England, the company offers a fully hosted and managed advanced voice service that enables enhanced capabilities for businesses of all sizes, including unified messaging, disaster recovery and flexible call routing via a user-friendly Web interface. Cox Business ranked highest among small/mid-size business data service providers in the J.D. Power and Associates 2010 U.S. Major Provider Business Telecommunications Study℠.

Cox Business is constantly expanding its service offerings beyond traditional voice, data and video products to provide customers with a full-service solution that meets the demands of today's business environment.

Online data backup, security, Web hosting and server protection services have been developed specifically for businesses requirements. For customers with server storage and disaster recovery concerns, we're expanding our data center facilities throughout Connecticut. For specific information about relocating critical business equipment to one of these facilities, please contact John Crouse at 860-432-5067.

Cox Business also offers Wi-Fi Hotspots — turn-key hotspot solutions for businesses looking to meet the increasing customer demand for Internet connectivity in public places. The Wi-Fi Hotspot network is growing rapidly in Connecticut.

All Cox Business services are delivered over the carrier-class, fully-owned and managed Cox network, ensuring the highest levels of security, quality and reliability. Cox Business customers experience the convenience of working with one local account team for all of their business telecommunications needs. Whether the business has a large in-house IT team or no on-site resources, Cox partners with its customers to ensure communications systems are optimized to support business operations.

Cox Business is the commercial service division of Cox Communications, a multi-service broadband communications and entertainment company with more than 6 million residential and business customers nationwide. Cox began providing business services in 1993 and has been an industry leader in serving businesses in New England since 1999 with a local team led by industry veteran Mark Scott, Vice President of Cox Business.

We believe our customers, vendors and business partners want to do business with socially and environmentally responsible organizations. Two initiatives encompass that objective: Cox Charities and Cox Conserves.

Cox Charities

Since its inception in 2001, Cox Communications has presented more than $5 million in Cox Charities grants and in-kind support to more than 130 nonprofit organizations focusing on children and educational initiatives in Rhode Island and Connecticut, including Girls Inc of Meriden. This year we will donate approximately $1.2 million in the form of Cox Charities grants and in-kind support to selected non-profit organizations in Rhode Island and Connecticut.

Cox Conserves

We're working to reduce our company's carbon footprint by 2017. Cox has implemented a range of programs that reduce energy use and promote sustainability, including the recycling of customer premise equipment, using hybrid vehicles in our fleet and the composting of food and materials from the cafeteria, which serves more than 625 meals per day.

Goodwin College

By giving their students an opportunity to gain a foothold in growing career fields, Goodwin College provides both an educational service and a boost to employers looking for qualified workers.

Goodwin College was founded in 1999 with the goal of transforming a small business technology training center into a regional force for economic development and educational access.

Within its first 10 years, Goodwin College garnered an impressive list of milestones, including the development of one of Connecticut's best nursing programs, approval to offer bachelor's degrees, and the construction of a new campus on the Connecticut River in East Hartford. Built on a remediated brownfield, the campus is often cited as the standard for smart growth and has won a host of design and environmental awards, including Project of the Year from the Northeastern Economic Developers Association, the leading economic development organization in the northeast.

While keeping an eye on a broader educational perspective, Goodwin has made a priority of catering to a student population that is often underserved in the state's higher education system. More than half of Goodwin's 3,000 attendees are first-generation college students and the student body reflects the diversity of the Hartford metropolitan area. The college's career-focused programs lead to strong employment outcomes for its graduates: More than 80 percent find employment in their chosen field or opt to advance their education.

Retaining at-risk students and placing them in the workforce requires and array of innovative student supports. Goodwin College's approaches are truly trend setting. Goodwin identifies and tracks the progress of students who are at risk of failing and employs a case-management approach which includes individualized counseling, advising and tutoring. For students facing financial hardships, the college operates its own food and diaper banks and providing below-market temporary housing for students in transition.

In line with its focus on student success, Goodwin aggressively seeks to leverage partnerships and grant opportunities to develop new programs aimed at college completion. One such program, Men of Vision and Education, or MOVE, is aimed squarely at one of the most vexing social problems facing the Hartford region — low rates of college completion among disadvantaged male students. The program, formed in partnership with the Hartford Foundation for Public Giving, is demonstrating that a case-management approach can help these students complete work for a college degree at a higher rate than their peers, despite serious challenges.

By giving these students an opportunity to gain a foothold in growing career fields, Goodwin College provides both an educational service and a boost to employers looking for qualified workers. By building the state's largest nursing program, for example, Goodwin has helped to alleviate what policymakers characterized as a critical shortage of trained nurses in the state. Other niche programs also have an impact. In 2009, Goodwin's training program in histology, a lab specialty related to cancer diagnoses, was No. 1 in

Above: Goodwin's riverfront campus in East Hartford has won awards for both design and environmental impact. Today, over 3,000 students attend classes at a site that was once a contaminated brownfield.

Below: Being a good neighbor is engrained in the culture of Goodwin. Pictured are volunteers from the 2010 Rebuilding Together community cleanup.

Over 80 percent of Goodwin graduates find jobs in their chosen fields, or continue their education. Goodwin grads are sought after by employers because of the specialized training they receive.

the nation in the performance of its students on the certifying exam. Not coincidentally, the program achieves 100-percent job placement every year, and is now being offered nationwide online.

Today, Goodwin is continuing its forward progression, having recently opened its first magnet high school — The Connecticut River Academy — with a second high school and an early childhood magnet school slated to open soon. With these new initiatives, Goodwin seeks to apply the same mission and innovative approaches that have been proven at the college level to younger students, providing cutting-edge, job-focused training combined with strong academics.

Also on the horizon is the continued development of the River Campus, with planners now weighing the possibility of adding student housing and new classroom buildings to support the school's growing enrollment. New academic focuses are being developed to meet market needs, including the development of environmental science programs and a new degree-completion program for working professionals.

What comes next for Goodwin College? Only time will tell, but one thing is for certain: the college will continue to strive to be as nimble as the marketplace to meet evolving demands. If there is one common theme that ties together the past, present, and future of this can-do college, it is the tendency to set big goals — so ambitious that some question their efficacy — and then, remarkably, achieve them, time and time again.

Goodwin's vision has won praise from all corners:

"Goodwin continually reinvents its curriculum to connect to available jobs."
– *Hartford Courant editorial, February 28, 2006*

"It is exciting to see an institution like Goodwin College that is on the frontlines of expanding not just access to education, but success in higher education."
– *Commissioner Michael Meotti, Department of Higher Education, at 2009 River Campus Dedication*

"Without vision, there can be no victory. This morning we celebrate both a great vision, and a great victory."
– *Congressman John Larson, at 2009 River Campus Dedication*

"In 10 years, Goodwin College has grown to become a respected institution providing educational opportunities to the underserved."
– *Connecticut Newsman Tom Monahan, at 2009 River Campus Dedication.*

Rider Productions LLC

A very unique full-service event management and production company, **Rider Productions** *helps make any event dynamic, memorable and successful.*

Above: Producers John & Sally Rider have over 40 years combined experience in the events and entertainment industry.

Below: The Connecticut Science Center 'Green Gala.'

For John and Sally Rider, founders of Rider Productions, there really is no business like corporate show business! They manage concerts, corporate sales rallies, the Connecticut Business Expo, the Western MA Business Expo, galas, awards ceremonies, networking functions and festivals. They have the depth and experience to handle top-draw public events as well as professionally and seamlessly execute all levels of corporate events.

John and Sally Rider bring a combined 40 years of event production and management to Rider Productions.

Now in its eighth year, Rider Productions has spanned the event globe in terms of the type of events they produce. Sally spent more than a dozen years coordinating corporate events for Fleet Bank before launching the company. John spent his professional life performing and producing rock concerts and shows across the country. As bass guitarist and founding member of Max Creek, one of New England's premier bands for over thirty years, he brings sophisticated, high-tech, audio-visual, lighting, staging and space design expertise to Rider Productions.

"I was corporate; John was rock 'n roll. It made sense to merge our talents," Sally says. "Our experiences help us meet a broad range of event objectives."

In addition to producing the event itself, Rider Productions offers involvement with the client from the very beginning of a project. Some of the specialized services Rider Productions offers are identifying event themes and messages, determining a budget, designing sponsor materials and assisting in site selection, logistics, décor and post-event follow up. "We are in fact a very unique full service event management and production company," says Sally. "Many times, companies hire us when they don't have their own internal event coordinator. We work with their staff to bring the elements of the event to fruition, letting their staff focus on other priorities."

Rider Productions has grown rapidly since 2003 and now produces and manages events throughout New England. Their top priority is to make sure that when a guest leaves a Rider-produced event, they know the message. They've felt it, seen it, tasted it, heard it and ultimately, are empowered by it!

"We are excellent at conveying the client's message to an audience. One way we do that is with video," she explains. The company's North Granby offices house a fully equipped, state-of-the art production studio. "We work with charities, CEOs, marketing teams, and all sorts of groups to create video documentaries and montages which can produce a very dynamic visual addition to any event."

Over the years, the Riders have been active supporters of local non-profit arts, civic and social services organizations. They are proud to manage the exciting 'Green Gala' at the Connecticut Science Center, and produce the Hartford Children's Theater 'Kid at Heart' Galas.

Rider Productions looks forward to many new and exciting events, in 2012 and beyond. The opening of 'The Hospital of the Future' at Baystate Medical Center is just an example of the diverse nature of Rider's expertise. When companies align with Rider Productions there's no limit to the event support they'll receive!

Above: Reach Foundation 'Reach Music Festival' featuring Earth, Wind & Fire.

Left: Hartford Children's Theater 'Kid at Heart' Gala.

Below: A painter-themed table at the Hartford Business Journal's Women In Business event.

Camilliere, Cloud & Kennedy

Camilliere, Cloud & Kennedy, based in West Hartford and Hartford, Connecticut, is a government relations, public affairs grassroots and business development firm that actively promotes legislative, administrative, and regulatory interests for our clients to garner favorable policy outcomes.

Our philosophy at Camilliere, Cloud & Kennedy is to work with a select number of clients to develop and implement government relations strategies that provide measurable results. When you hire Camilliere, Cloud & Kennedy, you work directly with the principals of the firm who have proven track records and experience working in a collaborative and bipartisan manner to obtain the results our clients expect.

The legislative services offered by Camilliere, Cloud & Kennedy include:

- Research, strategic planning, direct lobbying, drafting of and tracking of specific legislation.
- Issues/crisis management.
- Implementation of plans and strategies with the executive and legislative branches of government — as well as the congressional delegation — as they affect the interests of the client.
- Development and implementation of a public affairs and outreach program to deal with the electronic and print media.
- Issue intelligence gathering.
- Identification and mobilization of grassroots interest groups to support legislative goals.
- Bipartisan representation, coalition building and constituent mobilization.
- Development of strategies for enacting, implementing or defeating legislation or regulations.
- Attend hearings, conferences and meetings on behalf of the client.

Through relationships with elected officials and their staffs, as well as established affiliations with the business and trade association communities, Camilliere, Cloud & Kennedy has been successful in becoming an effective vehicle for legislative, administrative and regulatory initiatives.

With more than 50 years of collective legislative experience, Camilliere, Cloud & Kennedy has successfully represented clients in a variety of complex local as well as national issues such as transportation, health, energy, tobacco, international trade, education, gaming and construction. Our client list includes numerous well-known national corporations and organizations as well as small to medium-sized businesses and trade associations.

Camilliere, Cloud & Kennedy has earned a reputation as an effective and persuasive advocate in the municipal, state and federal arenas of government, which we are very proud to offer to all of our clients. We put our experience, relationships and reputations to work to provide ethical, effective and exceptional government relations services for our clients.

Anthony D. Camilliere, Principal. With nearly 15 years of government relations experience, Mr. Camilliere has represented and advocated on behalf of individuals and companies from the energy and utility, health care, financial, information technology, and tobacco industries, as well as, nonprofit organizations and real estate ventures. Strategic planning, crisis management, direct lobbying, and research legislation are his areas of expertise.

Mr. Camilliere started in public service as the executive assistant to the State Senate Majority Leader before moving into the role of executive assistant to the State Senate President Pro Tempore. His work included developing and tracking key legislation through the enactment process by working with members of the Senate caucus and House of Representatives. He also over saw the appointment process of all boards and commissions designated by state statute.

Mr. Camilliere holds a bachelor's degree from the University of Connecticut. He resides in Wethersfield, Connecticut, with his wife Anne and their two sons.

Christopher R. Cloud, Principal. Christopher R. Cloud is a principal with Camilliere, Cloud & Kennedy and also a partner in his family's real estate and business development firm called the Cloud Company, based in Hartford. Prior to joining the firm Mr. Cloud was founder and president of the Cloud Consulting Group, a lobbying and nonprofit consulting firm based in Hartford. Prior to that, Cloud served as president & CEO of AMISTAD America Inc., a non-profit organization which built, owned and operated the state of Connecticut's Official Flag Ship and Tall Ship Ambassador, Freedom Schooner Amistad. Mr. Cloud is a 1991 graduate of Howard University in Washington, D.C.

Cloud and his wife Stacy reside in Farmington, Connecticut, with their twin sons Prescott and Sanford.

Brendan J. Kennedy, Principal. In addition to his role

Chris Cloud, left, and Tony Camilliere & provide clients with a wealth of experience in government relations, grassroots & business development.

as a principal with Camilliere, Cloud & Kennedy, Mr. Kennedy is a partner in a national firm comprised of the nation's premier grassroots and public affairs campaign managers. The National Field Resource Network provides politically sophisticated corporations, trade associations and lobbyists with an efficient source for generating grassroots and public affairs action on legislative issues.

He holds a bachelor's degree in political science as well was a master's degree in education. Mr. Kennedy resides in New Britain, Connecticut, with his wife Raquel.

Ashley M. Calabrese, Associate. Ms. Calabrese began working at Camilliere, Cloud & Kennedy as an intern during the 2010 legislative session. She has since joined the firm as a full-time lobbyist. Ms. Calabrese provides direct lobbying as well as administrative work, legislative research and client management. She specializes in all issues regarding insurance and health care.

Ms. Calabrese graduated with a bachelor's in psychology from Connecticut College. She resides in Roxbury, Connecticut.

Michael Caron, Associate. Mr. Caron comes to CCK with more than 20 years of experience in the public policy arena. He recently worked as the director of public affairs-global sites at Pfizer's Research & Development sites in Groton, New London and New Haven, Connecticut. He worked as a member of Pfizer's Groton/New London leadership team and was Pfizer's congressional site captain. Before joining Pfizer, Mr. Caron served nine terms in the Connecticut General Assembly as a member of the House of Representatives, where he was assistant minority leader representing Canterbury, Killingly, Plainfield and Sterling in northeastern Connecticut. Michael Caron resides in West Hartford, Connecticut, with his wife Maureen.

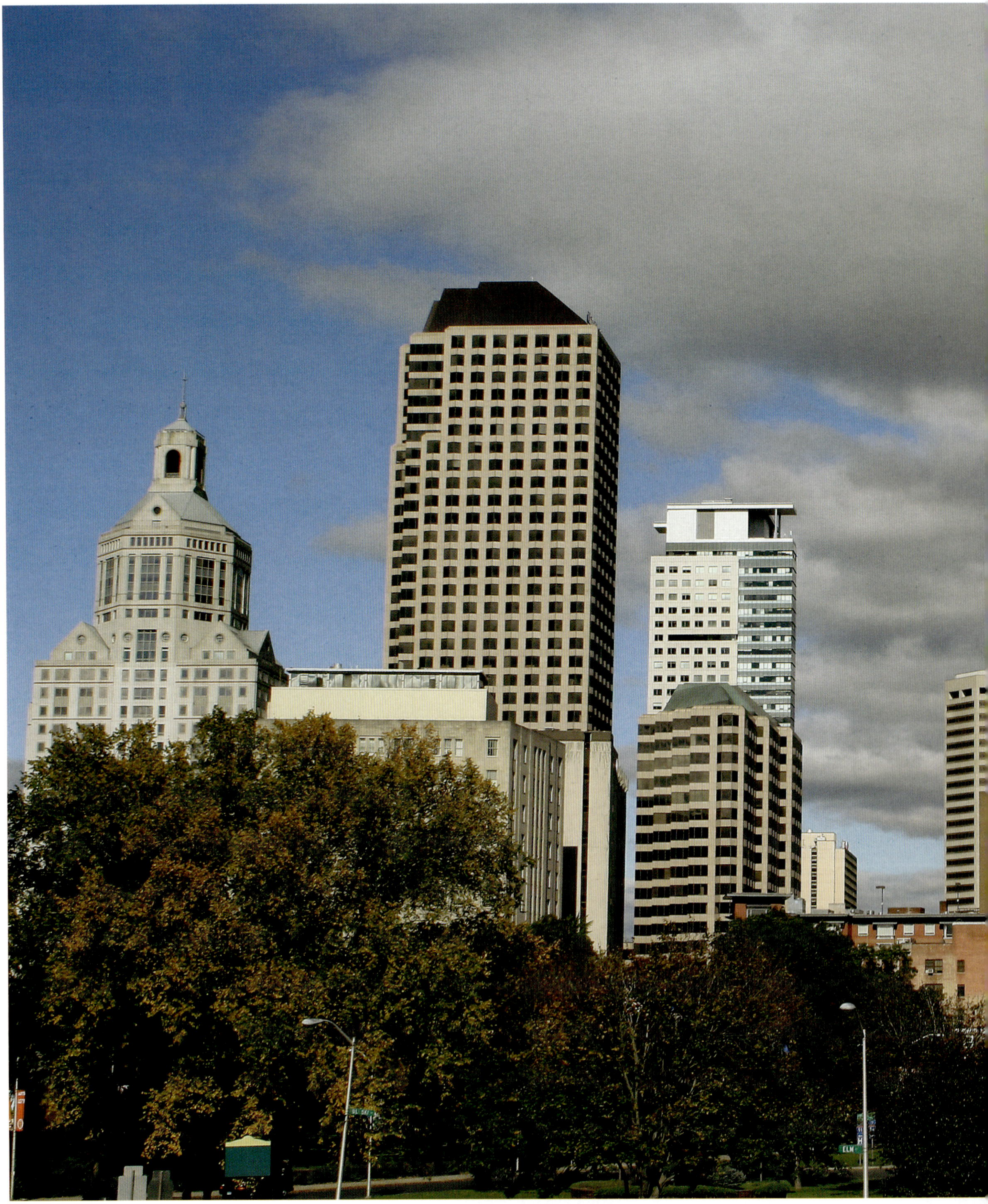

PHOTOGRAPHIC MOMENTS

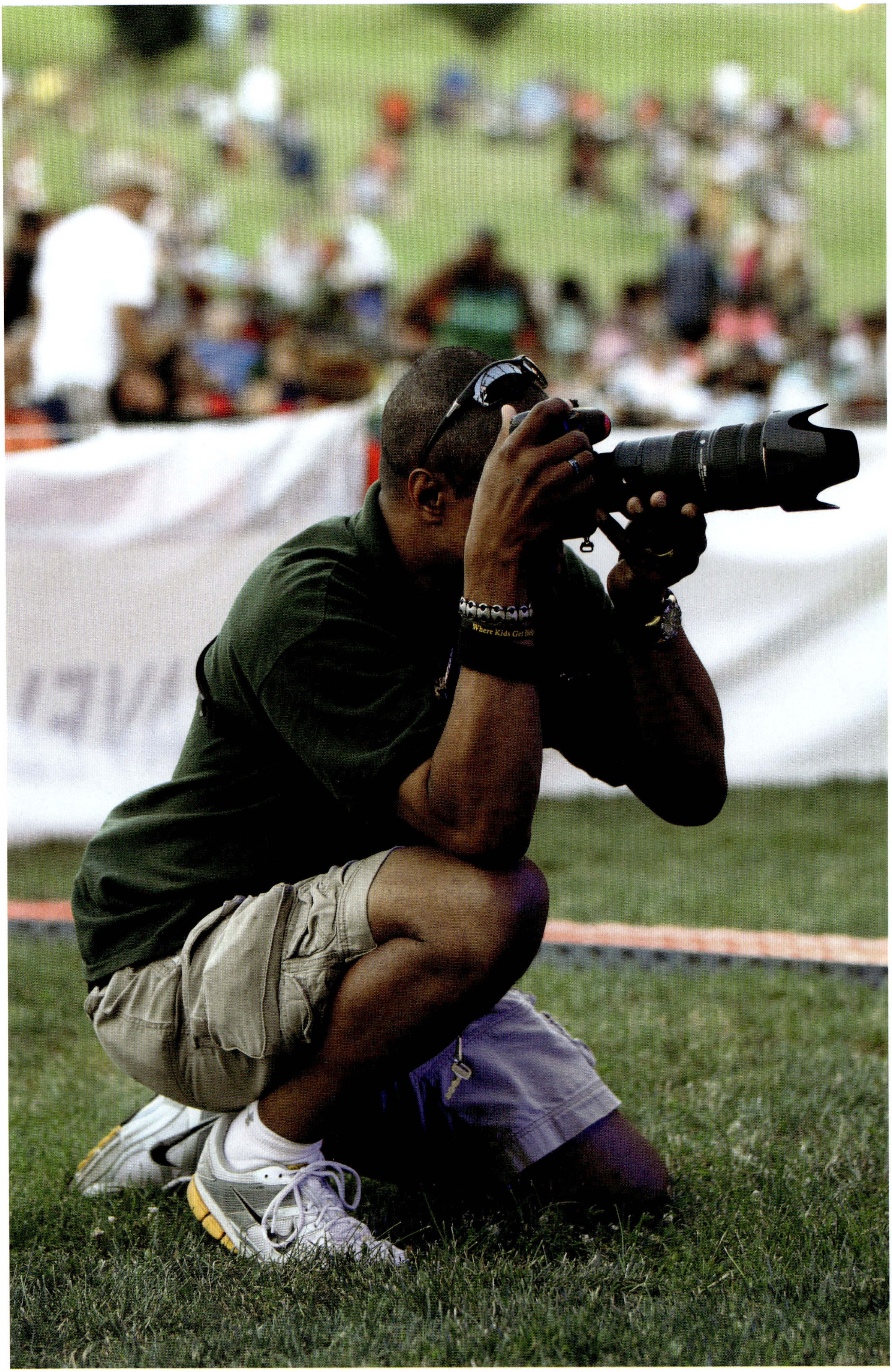

DAVID NEWMAN

Photographers

LEONARD HELLERMAN is well known for his artistic nature and landscape photography that uses advanced digital techniques. Hellerman is a longtime member and current president of the Connecticut Academy of Fine Arts. In the winter months, he serves as the staff photographer for the Palm Beach Photographic Centre in Delray Beach, Fla., where he also assists with classes and workshops. His imagery is on permanent display in many businesses and institutions in Greater Hartford and he has photographs in the permanent collections of the New Britain Museum of American Art and the William Benton Museum of Art of the University of Connecticut.

ANDY HART grew up in Hartford's Blue Hills neighborhood. He began his career in journalism in 1989 as a reporter for the Glastonbury Citizen. Like most small-town newspapers, the Citizen required its reporters to shoot their own photos and Andy discovered he had a knack for the art. In 1992, he began working for the Hartford News in Hartford's South End. Over the years, Andy has worked there as a reporter, photographer, advertising salesman, art director, delivery boy and janitor. He has photographed thousands of Hartford events in the past two decades, with a particular emphasis on showcasing Hartford's rich diversity of ethnic groups and nationalities.

EVA GRYK is a resident of New Britain. She has won numerous awards in the former New Britain Camera Club, local fairs, Greater Lynn International Color Exhibition, CT Association of Photographers and at the annual juried Joy of Art Show at Hospital for Special Care. In 2008, Eva was an Honorable Mention Winner in the Popular Photography Magazine Annual Readers' International Photo competition, and in 2010 was a First Place Award Winner in the same Popular Photography Magazine contest. One of her prints was accepted into the Members Show at the New Britain Museum of American Art in 2010 and sold at auction during the museum's Annual Gala Art Party of the Year. Eva's published work has appeared in many books, most recently "Rum Runners, Governors, Beachcombers & Socialists —Views of the Beaches in Old Lyme."

DAVID B. NEWMAN is a freelance photographer and photojournalist and a life-long resident of West Hartford, CT. Galleries of his work can be viewed at www.PhotoByNewman.com.

JENNIFER FIERECK decided to turn her hobby into a career and continue a family tradition after photographing her best friend's wedding ten years ago. In 2006, Jennifer and her husband, Dave, founded J. Fiereck Photography, which specializes in weddings and commercial projects, in addition to offering traditional portraits and event photography. J. Fiereck clients include Connecticut Children's Medical Center, CT Convention Center, Hartford Business Journal and Saint Francis Hospital. J. Fiereck Photography is also the proud recipient of a 2011 WeddingWire Bride's Choice Award, as well as being named a 2011 The Knot Best of Weddings Pick, which are both based on reviews by local brides. Jennifer is a Certified Professional Photographer and a graduate of the University of Connecticut with a degree in Marketing/Communications. More info is available at www.jfiereck.com.

CHARLENE MCMAHON is a freelance photographer and writer. She has done photography for a C-Span publication, AOL Patch, Imprint Newspapers, the New Britain Herald, the Bristol Press, the Hartford Symphony, and Camp Courant. Her photos have been on exhibit at the Canton Gallery on the Green, the West Hartford Art League, and the Discovery Museum in Bridgeport.

JOHN MURPHY has had an interest in photography for many years, but only became serious about pursuing his passion in 2003. Since the beginning of 2004, he has worked exclusively with digital imaging. John has been a member of the New Britain Camera Club, the New Haven Camera Club and the Charter Oak Photographic Society which he currently serves as President. He has competed in many local and regional photography competitions and has won numerous awards. Most recently, his "Another Slot Shot" was named the Traditional Color Print of the Year at the Charter Oak Photographic Society's annual competition John has had his work displayed at the West Hartford Art League and the Art League of New Britain as well as the New Britain Museum of American Art's Juried Shows and the Hospital for Special Care's "Joy of Art" shows.

STEVE LASCHEVER has been working as a photographer for a quarter-century. He has become renowned for the warmth of his portraits of local personalities and his ability to capture the significant moment in the life of a person or community. His work has appeared in publications and on walls throughout Connecticut. More information is available at his website: www.laschphoto.com

KIM KNOX BECKIUS is a Connecticut-based travel writer and photographer. Since 1998, she has produced About.com's New England Travel Web site, taking readers from around the world on virtual tours of New England, providing travel inspiration and sharing insight into Yankee tradition, history and ingenuity. Her seventh book, "New England's Historic Homes & Gardens," was published in 2011. Her writing and photography have also been featured on several other travel-related Web sites and in magazines. She regularly interacts with travelers on Twitter: @newenglandgirl. More info at http://gonewengland.about.com.

PABLO ROBLES is the founder of Media Compass, a Massachusetts based company. An accomplished photojournalist, his work appears regularly in the Hartford Business Journal. He has also been a photographer for the Middletown Press as well as a photographer and photo editor for the New Haven Register's Spanish-language magazine "Registro." More info available at www.mediacompass.org.

LISA MIKULSKI is a freelance writer, designer and photographer presently living in Westbrook, Conn. She has devoted the last 10 years to working in the arts industry and promoting artists, designers, and art organizations. She says, "My sensibilities are drawn toward color, texture, line, light and shadow... always light, but sometimes also the lack of light and how that can effect the subject. I can't explain how I went from being the gal who would cut off the heads of my loved ones in photos to someone who is able to capture a moment or a surprise in time and share it with a community. See www.lisamikulski.com for more info.

Other photographers featured in Hartford: Photographic Moments are: **ALEX BERNSTEIN, SALLY ROTHENHAUS, LAWRENCE ROY, NICK CAITO, MARK RUGGIERO, DREW GIBSON, KEITH GRIFFIN, LYNN MIKA, KAREN O'MAXFIELD AND CAILIN EMMETT.**

Company Index

Company Name	Contact Information	Page Number
Aetna	www.aetna.com	146
Ahlstrom	www.ahlstrom.com	130
Camilliere, Cloud & Kennedy	www.cckgov.com	200
Capewell Components Company LLC	www.capewell.com	157
Carousel Industries	www.carouselindustries.com	188
Channel 3 Kids Camp	www.channel3kidscamp.org	168
Charles Wareham and Associates/LPL Financial	www.LPL.com/Charles.Wareham	190
Charter Oak Insurance and Financial Services Company	www.charteroakfinancial.com	160
Cigna	www.cigna.com	134
Cox Business	www.coxbusiness.com	195
Goodwin College	www.goodwin.edu	196
Hartford Business Journal	www.hartfordbusiness.com	191
Hartford Courant – CT1 Media	www.ct1media.com	126
Hartford Hospital	www.harthosp.org	150
Hartford Public Library	www.hplct.org	132
Horton International LLC	www.hortoninternational.com	182
LAZ Parking	www.lazparking.com	184
McCarter & English, LLP	www.mccarter.com	144
MetroHartford Alliance	www.metrohartford.com	136
Northeast Utilities	www.nu.com	158
Nutmeg State Federal Credit Union	www.nutmegstatefcu.org	172
Oakleaf Waste Management	www.oakleafwaste.com	192
Prudential Retirement	www.prudential.com	154
PwC	www.pwc.com	145
Rider Productions LLC	www.riderevents.com	198
Saint Francis Hospital and Medical Center	www.stfranciscare.org	162
Saint Joseph College	www.sjc.edu	170
Stanley Black & Decker	www.stanleyblackanddecker.com	140
Stockton Associates		183
Suburban Companies	www.suburbancompanies.com	177
The Associated Construction Company	www.accgc.com	174
The City of Hartford	www.hartford.gov	122
The Governor's Prevention Partnership	www.preventionworksct.org	186
The Hartford	www.thehartford.com	138
The Hartford Club	www.hartfordclub.com	153
The Simon Konover Company	www.simonkonover.com	176
The Town and County Club	www.towncounty.com	169
UnitedHealth Group	www.uhc.com	180
TRUMPF Inc.	www.us.trumpf.com	178
University of Hartford	www.hartford.edu	156

Alex Bernstein